EXPERIENCING SACRED COMMUNITY

GILA GEVIRTZ

**TORAH AURA
PRODUCTIONS**

· ·

Dedicated to:

Kate, Ilan, Yoni, Shira and Rhoda

because sacred community begins with family and friends.

· ·

ISBN 10: 1–934527–71–8

ISBN 13: 978–1–934527–71–9

Copyright © 2013 Gila Gevirtz.

Published by Torah Aura Productions. All rights reserved.

No part of this publication may be reproduced or transmitted in any form or by any means graphic, electronic or mechanical, including photocopying, recording or by any information storage and retrieval system, without permission in writing from the publisher.

Torah Aura Productions • 4423 Fruitland Avenue, Los Angeles, CA 90058

(800) BE-Torah • (800) 238-6724 • (323) 585-7312 • fax (323) 585-0327

E-MAIL <misrad@torahaura.com> • Visit the Torah Aura website at www.torahaura.com

Manufactured in China

Table of Contents

What Is a Jewish Sacred Community?

Kehillah Kedoshah קְהִלָּה קְדוֹשָׁה

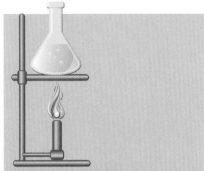

EXPERiENCE

MISSION IMPOSSIBLE?

Some challenges, like chess games, require mental smarts. Others, like juggling, call for physical skill. Here's a brainteaser that demands a bit of both.

Standing in a circle with your classmates, hold a *kippah* in one hand while keeping both arms straight. The challenge is to get the *kippah* on your head without bending either elbow. If after several tries you want a clue, read the Jewish folktale on the right.

Walking through a magnificent palace, a man came upon a group of people seated at a table, sobbing. Although food and drink were generously laid out, not even a morsel reached their lips, for they could not bend their elbows. Moving to the next room, the man came upon another group of people who also could not bend their elbows. Yet these people were savoring the feast before them. Reaching out to their neighbors, they fed one another and rejoiced.

- Based on the folktale, what is the most efficient—perhaps only—way to solve the brainteaser?
- When did you realize that you had to collaborate with your classmates?
- What else have you worked on with others—for example, volunteer programs, class reports or school plays?
- What were the benefits of collaboration?
- What were the challenges?

ACTIVITY

What's the Value?

The communities you choose to be active in reveal a lot about you and what you value.

Below, list three communities that are important to you. Describe why you value each one and what you contribute to it.

1. family

_____

2. Sports

_____

3. _____

_____

Describe an additional community you would like to join or create and why.

_____

_____

_____

Share these insights with a partner.

As we grow and mature, no matter how much we enjoy time alone or how capable and independent we become, we still need other people—and not just one or two, but lots of people, whole communities—to help us live full and rewarding lives.

We join different communities—synagogues, schools, clubs, volunteer organizations and gamer communities. Each provides at least one benefit, if not many—friendship, emotional support, education or fun. Each asks for something in return—respect, cooperation, loyalty, time or effort.

What Makes a Community Sacred?

A community is defined most by its purpose or reason for being. For example, the purpose of a varsity football team is to develop members' athletic skills and sportsmanship. That is why a coach trains the team, not a scientist or ballet dancer, and why members wear helmets and padding, not lab coats or tutus.

Clique versus Community

People who share values or interests may form a community of friends or a clique. Working in small groups, discuss how the two social groups differ. For example, compare and contrast the purpose, characteristics and benefits of a community of friends versus a clique.

EXPERiENCE

Imagine that several teens have formed a clique. Some are happy with the group as it is; others want it to be more like a community of friends. Role-play a discussion in which teens with opposing views try to persuade one another to change their preference. Afterward, as a class, discuss the issues that came up and how they relate to your real-life experience.

Like all communities, the Jewish community has a purpose. Its reason for being is to honor the Covenant, or *Brit*, our agreement to fulfill the *mitzvot* (plural of *mitzvah*) so that we can live as a holy people, or an *am kadosh*. But what does it mean to be a holy people when Judaism teaches that *all* life is holy?

True, our tradition teaches that God made all Creation holy. However, being a holy people means picking up where God left off. When we are generous, respectful and compassionate to others, we follow in God's ways, adding holiness to the world. When we care for the sick and the hungry and conserve the earth's resources, we use our God-given holiness to create yet more holiness. And when we celebrate Shabbat we not only honor Creation but also add to its holiness.

EXPERiENCE

I COULD DIE!

Work in a small group.

Have you ever heard someone say, "I'm so embarrassed, I could die"? If you have, you will understand this teaching: "A person who publicly humiliates a neighbor is, as it were, guilty of murder."

Do you think this teaching was inspired by secular or by Jewish law? Why?

Jewish law: the quote is from the Talmud, Bava M'tzia 58b

EXPERiENCE

LAUNCH A PEER PROMO

Imagine that you are on a PR team that is promoting the value of Jewish community among teens. Your responsibility is to help your peers understand how sacred acts can help them enjoy life *and* make the world a better place.

Consider the words you want to use. Would the word *mitzvah* inspire or turn off your peers? Why? If you prefer not to use that word, how else could you express the concept of sacred acts? Why do you think that would be more acceptable to your peers?

Working in a small group, brainstorm a list of *mitzvot* you think would be of interest to and inspire teens—for example, pursuing justice or reciting a blessing. Include two such actions in your promo, which you can create as a poster or digital video or audio recording.

When your group completes its project, you may share it with your class and seek permission to post it on your synagogue's website or Facebook page. As a class you may want to fulfill two *mitzvot* from among those that you promoted.

ACTIVITY

Sacred Community in Action: Jewish Federations of North America

Caring for the world is a big job. That's why the Jewish community created a network of organizations to help us help others. The largest of these is the Jewish Federations of North America (JFNA). One of the top ten charities on the continent, it includes 157 Jewish federations and more than 300 Jewish communities.

JFNA serves people in sixty countries, including the United States, Canada and Israel. It helps fund synagogues, Jewish schools, Jewish community centers (JCCs) and Hillels on college campuses. It also works to feed, clothe and house people in need and provides financial assistance and medical and trauma relief to victims of natural disasters.

JFNA gains much of its strength from teaming up with others. For example, in 2010 it joined Teens United for Haiti, a T-shirt fundraising project launched by several Jewish youth groups. It also partners with the Jewish Agency and Joint Distribution Committee to help Ethiopians and other oppressed Jewish communities rebuild their lives in Israel.

JFNA promotes hands-on volunteerism and group action.

- Why are these characteristics essential to a sacred community?

- Describe another characteristic of a *kehillah kedoshah* that you think is essential and why.

Your Class Can Be a Kehillah Kedoshah

Aspiring actors or baseball players don't go straight to Broadway or the major leagues. First they learn the basic skills; then they practice, practice, practice and gain experience. When they reach their goals, they develop more advanced skills, which they practice until they are ready for the next level.

Your classroom is also your training ground. At its best, it builds solidarity and strength, helping you create a *kehillah kedoshah* where people share fun experiences and a sense of belonging, study and pray together, and treat one another with respect, working collaboratively for the benefit of all.

EXPERiENCE

YEAH! WE'VE GOT COMMUNITY

To express the spirit and values of your *kehillah kedoshah,* create a class motto to put on a banner, mural or T-shirts or to include in a class cheer or song. You can work in teams to develop ideas, then vote on an official motto. You can also work in teams to create a song, banner and cheer. To help you warm up and get your imagination going, you may want to brainstorm words that describe your class.

Consider if you want to base your motto on traditional sources or to write an original one. One classic saying that could work is Hillel's teaching:

אִם אֵין אֲנִי לִי, מִי לִי? וּכְשֶׁאֲנִי לְעַצְמִי, מָה אֲנִי?

"If I am not for myself, who will be for me? If I am only for myself, what am I?" *(Pirkei Avot 1:14).*

• How would you express Hillel's beliefs in your own words?

When you have completed your work, shout out, sing, display or wear your creations, perhaps inviting your principal and rabbi to enjoy them with you.

<u>H</u>evruta and Midrash

Like prayer, Bible study is essential to building Jewish sacred communities. Two study tools that may be new to you are <u>h</u>evruta partnerships and *midrash*.

<u>H</u>evruta is a traditional form of peer study in which two students read sacred text together and discuss—even respectfully argue about—its meaning.

By sharing their beliefs and views, *<u>h</u>evruta* partners can contribute to each other's understanding of sacred text. "I have learned much from my teachers, but even more from my partner," said Rabbi <u>H</u>anina (Ta'anit 7a). What have you learned from your peers? What have you taught them?

The second tool, *midrash*, is the ancient storytelling tradition that helps explain the Bible's lessons and fills in missing information. For example, the Torah does not describe our patriarch Abraham's youth, so our Rabbis stepped in and created a *midrash* about how as a young adult Abraham's belief in God motivated him to smash the idols in his father's shop. *Experiencing Sacred Community* will invite you to create *midrash* to personalize and deepen your experience and understanding of Jewish texts and values.

Creating a *kehillah kedoshah* can be an exciting, fun-filled adventure. It also can require work. Yet it's worth the effort. When done with an open mind and heart, it can help you explore your identity, values and beliefs. It can strengthen and enrich you, broaden your circle of friends and teach you how to add holiness to the world.

Do Not Set Yourself Apart from the Community

Sometimes, even in the strongest communities, problems may arise that tempt us to back off or completely walk away. But Jews are asked to resist such impulses and work through the challenges. As our sage Hillel taught, "Do not separate yourself from the community" (*Pirkei Avot 2:5*).

EXPERiENCE

LET'S TALK ABOUT IT: THE SCROLL OF ESTHER 4:12–14

Reread the *Megillat Esther* text on the right with a <u>hevruta</u> partner. Take turns reading aloud, and in your own words, explain why Mordecai thinks Esther should help the Jews. Do you think he is being fair? After all, to approach the king without an invitation would put Esther's life at risk.

Just as Genesis does not describe Abraham's youth, the *megillah* does not describe Esther's upbringing, other than to say she was an orphan. Create a *midrash* about Esther's childhood that illustrates the seeds of her commitment to community. Your *midrash* can be in the form of a story, poem or picture.

Consider tapping into your personal experience to create the *midrash*. Was there a time when you wanted to walk away from your classmates or a group of friends but decided to remain? Why did you stay?

Be prepared to share your *midrash* with the class and to discuss how it can help us understand why, as an adult, Esther risks everything to save her people.

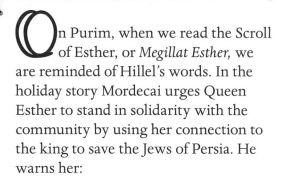

On Purim, when we read the Scroll of Esther, or *Megillat Esther,* we are reminded of Hillel's words. In the holiday story Mordecai urges Queen Esther to stand in solidarity with the community by using her connection to the king to save the Jews of Persia. He warns her:

> Do not imagine that, of all the Jews, you will escape with your life because you are in the king's palace. On the contrary, if you remain silent at this time, relief and deliverance for the Jews will arise from somewhere else, while you…perish. And who knows? You may have attained a royal position for [the sake of helping our people in] a crisis like this. (Esther 4:12–14).

ACTIVITY

Jacob Henry Schiff (1874–1920)

Our tradition teaches that "When the community is in trouble, one should not say, 'I will go to my house and eat and drink and be at peace with myself'" (*Ta'anit* 11a). Jacob Henry Schiff was a successful New York banker, a star in international finance and politics. He could have spent his free time hanging out with the rich and famous. But when the community was in trouble, Schiff was not at peace. Instead, he did what he could to help.

Schiff gave time and money to the oppressed Jews of Russia who suffered under the tsar. He founded New York's Montefiore Hospital and contributed to the Henry Street Settlement, which provides those in need with educational and health care services to this day. He also helped establish the Reform rabbinical seminary (Hebrew Union College) and Conservative seminary (Jewish Theological Seminary) and the Jewish Division in the New York Public Library. In addition, Schiff gave generously to the Technical Institute of Haifa in Israel (Technion); he funded Jewish education and also gave to secular humanitarian and cultural organizations such as the American Red Cross and the American Museum of Natural History.

- How might Schiff be compared to Queen Esther?

  _____

  _____

- Knowing what Schiff did as an adult, what qualities might he have had as a teen?

  _____

  _____

- Why do you think so?

  _____

  _____

Our sage Rabbi Simeon ben Yoḥai knew that even if we want to separate ourselves from the community, it's often impossible. He taught this lesson through *midrash*. As you read the *midrash,* think about what the boat and its passengers symbolize.

> Several passengers were on a boat at sea when one took a drill and began to bore a hole under his seat. Alarmed, his companions cried out, "What are you doing?"
>
> "What is it to you?" the man responded. "Am I not making the hole under *my* seat?"
>
> "But the water that comes in will sink the boat and drown us all," they retorted
>
> (*Leviticus Rabbah* 4:6, based on Numbers 16:22).

In real life, what personal choices might an individual make that have an impact—good or bad—on the larger community? Have you ever been affected by such choices? If yes, what was the impact? How did you respond?

At the heart of a *kehillah kedoshah* is the understanding that we're all in the same boat and must contribute to its care and to the welfare of its passengers. *Experiencing Sacred Community* will help you learn to do your part and to enjoy the journey. It will teach you how to create sacred community and how to harness its power to add goodness to the world and meaning and value to your life.

EXPERiENCE YOUR SACRED COMMUNiTY iN ACTiON

Choose one activity.

FAMILY LIFE AND LAW

Discuss whether your family rules have more in common with Jewish or American laws and values. For example, do they define minimum standards of behavior (like American law) or encourage helpfulness, respect and generosity (like Jewish law)?

LOCAL HEROES

Every synagogue has its local heroes, people who contribute to its welfare and growth above and beyond the call of duty. They tirelessly volunteer to usher at Shabbat services, visit the sick or invite new members to their homes; they give *tzedakah* generously and take the time to help and comfort others. With a partner, interview one or two such heroes in your synagogue to learn what motivates their generosity and what the challenges and rewards are. Then share with your class what you have learned. (You may want to invite the heroes to your presentation.)

WORLD WIDE WEB OF JEWS

To learn more about other Jewish communities, search the Web for electronic publications that can keep you updated on the latest ideas and news from Jews around the country and world. Your teacher, rabbi, cantor or synagogue librarian can help you. Also, you may want to partner with a parent to do your online searches. Report back to your class about a Jewish community that is based in another state, province or country.

Friendship
Yedidut יְדִידוּת

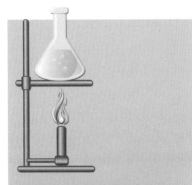

EXPERiENCE

Discuss this with a partner, then with your whole class.

Centuries before anyone texted BFFs, our ancestors sent shout-outs to friends. They declared that we don't just need friends; we need *close* friends, *great* friends, *soul-mate* friends! Our Rabbis boldly proclaimed that our best teachers are our friends, and that our best friends may be more loyal and precious than family.

Do you agree or disagree? Why? What do you think your friends, teachers and parents think? Why?

What Do Good Friends Do?

Judaism takes friendship seriously. It not only encourages friends to enjoy one another and to celebrate happy occasions together, it also urges them to be generous, compassionate, supportive and loyal confidants. "Two are better than one," says the Bible. "If they fall, one friend can raise the other. But woe to the person who is alone and falls…" (Ecclesiastes 4:9–10). Do you think the Bible is referring only to literally falling? What other meanings might there be?

16

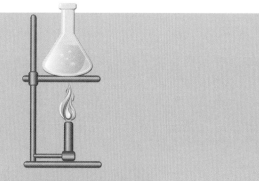

EXPERiENCE

LET'S TALK ABOUT IT: SAMUEL I 18:1-4

Working with a *hevruta* partner, reread the text from Samuel I. Take turns reading aloud. Discuss what it means to love a friend as yourself. Brainstorm actions that reflect this type of love. Discuss how far you would go to help a good friend. Consider why you would or would not promise, "Whatever you say, I will do for you." Based on your discussion, write a pact with your partner that you might make with your dearest friend.

Samuel I tells what Jonathan gave to David, but it doesn't say if David gave Jonathan anything. In the tradition of filling in missing information by creating *midrash*, develop a ceremony with your partner in which David and Jonathan make their pact and exchange gifts. You can base the pact on the one you wrote. Practice the ceremony and present it to your class.

According to the *Tanakh,* a good friend will protect you and give you the shirt—or cloak—off his or her back. We see this in the story of David and his best friend Jonathan (King Saul's son). Before David became king of Israel, Saul threatened to kill him. Deciding that blood is not always thicker than water, Jonathan disregarded his father's wishes and saved David's life.

> Jonathan's soul was bound with David's soul; Jonathan loved David as himself…. Jonathan and David made a pact because of his love for [David] as himself. Jonathan took off the cloak he was wearing and gave it to David along with his sword, his bow and his belt…. Jonathan said to David, "Whatever you say, I will do for you."

(Samuel I 18:1–4, 20:4)

ACTIVITY

Words of Friendship

In Jewish life, one word is not enough to capture the importance of a good friend. In fact, the *Tanakh* uses three different Hebrew words, each of which also means "beloved".

A יָדִיד *yadid* (male friend) and יְדִידָה *yedidah* (female friend) enjoy יְדִידוּת *yedidut* (friendship). On Friday nights and festivals we chant a prayer that calls God our Soul-mate Friend, יְדִיד-נֶפֶשׁ *Yedid Nefesh*. Similarly, in the Bible God describes us as "the friendship of My soul יְדִידוּת-נַפְשִׁי *yedidut nafshi*" (Jeremiah 12:7). What might our relationship with God have in common with our best friendships? How might knowing that guide your choice of friends?

Another word for friend is חָבֵר *haver* (male friend) or חֲבֵרָה *haveirah* (female friend). It is built on the root ח *het*, ב *vet*, ר *resh*. Words built on that root have meanings related to being connected or united. חֲבֵרוּת *Haveirut* (friendship), חֶבְרָה *hevrah* (social network) and חַבְרוּתָא *hevruta* are all built on the root ח *het*, ב *vet*, ר *resh*. What do the terms *friendship*, *social network*, and *study partner* have in common?

A third word for friend is רֵעַ *rei'a* (male friend) or רֵעָה *rei'ah* (female friend). רֵעָה *Rei'ah* also means "bride" and "wife". Sometimes it refers to the Jewish people. Who is the רֵעַ *rei'a* when רֵעָה *rei'ah* refers to the Jewish people? Why do you think so?

Cleaving to Friends

Friends can help us learn about a lot of things, including sports, music, foreign languages and technology. They can also help us learn to become compassionate, honest, peace-loving and kind. In fact, Jewish tradition emphasizes the role of peers, along with that of parents and teachers, in helping us develop a strong ethical and moral character.

Good friends reach out to catch us when we fall or go off track. They applaud us when we overcome challenges and achieve new goals, and they encourage us when we feel insecure or fearful. Good friends accept that we are imperfect, and—without judging us—they inspire us to improve. That is why our Rabbis list "cleaving to friends," or *dibuk haveirim* (*Pirkei Avot 6:6*), as one of the forty-eight virtues necessary for acquiring the wisdom of Torah. Indeed, much of the Torah's wisdom is about living in friendship with others.

The importance of *dibuk haveirim* is portrayed in the story of Ruth (whose name רות literally means "friend") and her mother-in-law Naomi. Jewish tradition honors Ruth as a convert to Judaism and as the great-grandmother of King David. Born a Moabite, she cleaves to Naomi in order to learn the sacred ways of the Israelite community.

> Ruth cleaved to [Naomi].… She said, "Do not urge me to leave you, to turn back from following you. For wherever you go, I will go; wherever you stay, I will stay; your people will be my people, and your God my God." (Ruth 1:14–16)

EXPERiENCE

LET'S TALK ABOUT IT: RUTH 1:14–16

Working with a *hevruta* partner, reread the text from Ruth. Take turns reading aloud. Discuss what might have motivated Ruth to follow Naomi and to embrace her people, land and God. What concerns might Naomi have expressed? What do you think Ruth said that persuaded Naomi to accept her?

With your *hevruta* partner, create a "living statue" that symbolizes *dibuk haveirim*. Use your bodies and available props. Consider the traits you want the statue to portray—for example, compassion, respect, loyalty and dignity. When everyone is ready, have each group present its statue. Invite the class to talk about the traits the statues reflect—not only how they contribute to friendship, but also how they can strengthen sacred communities.

Just as we are urged to cleave to good friends so, too, we are taught to cleave to God. Psalm 63:9 declares, "My soul cleaves to You [God]." Given that God is not a physical presence, what might it mean to cleave to God?

ACTIVITY

Making Sacred Meaning

Our Rabbis were so passionate about friendship that the Talmud, (books of Jewish law) instructs us to recite the *Sheheheyanu* blessing when we see a friend for the first time in thirty days—for example, after summer vacation or an illness.

בָּרוּךְ אַתָּה יי אֱלֹהֵינוּ מֶלֶךְ הָעוֹלָם שֶׁהֶחֱיָנוּ וְקִיְּמָנוּ וְהִגִּיעָנוּ לַזְּמַן הַזֶּה.

Praised are You, our God, Ruler of the universe, Who has given us life, kept us going, and brought us to this moment.

Upon seeing a friend for the first time in a year or more it is a tradition to recite the following blessing.

בָּרוּךְ אַתָּה יי אֱלֹהֵינוּ מֶלֶךְ הָעוֹלָם מְחַיֶּה הַמֵּתִים.

Praised are You, our God, Ruler of the universe, Who revives the dead.

Respond to the questions below and be prepared to share your answers with your class.

What might "revives the dead" mean? _____

_____

_____

What do the blessings express about the Jewish view of friendship? _____

_____

_____

EXPERiENCE

THANK GOD FOR FRIENDS!

Working with a partner, write a blessing to recite upon seeing a friend for the first time in a week. Before you begin, think about how you feel when you see friends after a period of absence. Also consider how you want your friend to feel on hearing your words.

Although you will write the blessing in English, begin with the traditional opening:

בָּרוּךְ אַתָּה יי אֱלֹהֵינוּ מֶלֶךְ הָעוֹלָם

Barukh Attah Adonai, Eloheinu, Melekh ha-Olam

_____

_____

_____

To build a feeling of sacred community, your class may want to recite one of the blessings when it meets each week. The class can also create a ritual to go with the blessing. For example, each student can contribute a pinch of cloves and cinnamon to a spice container (like one used for *havdalah*). When reciting the blessing you can pass around the container for everyone to smell its spices, symbolizing the idea that your friendships have revived you as a community.

The Bible says, "There are friends who keep us company, and there is a friend who cleaves and is more devoted than a sibling" (Proverbs 18:24). This proverb suggests that not all friendships must or can be at the level of *dibuk haveirim*. Do you agree or disagree? Why? What is the value of good companions? What is the added value of a friend who cleaves? What is the difference between a needy friend and a friend who cleaves?

21

As a group, then as a class, brainstorm and record ideas for the most important character traits one should look for in a good friend. When you have a list that includes everyone's ideas, invite your classmates to vote on the top ten traits of a good friend based on the list. The ten traits that receive the most votes will be your class's top ten.

As a way to contribute to your school's *kehillah kedoshah,* you can present your list of traits to a class of younger students, giving everyday examples of each one. Ask your audience if they agree that the traits are important and why. Invite the students to suggest additional traits they think are important.

The Character Traits of Good Friends

When the Hebrew letters ר *resh* and ע *ayin* come together without their vowels it's impossible to know if the word they form is רֵעַ *rei'a* (friend) or רַע *ra* (evil). It is the vowels that distinguish one word from the other. Like those vowels, character traits are what determine if the relationship two people form becomes a friendship or a source of evil.

The Talmud counsels us to choose friends wisely because *dibuk haveirim* is valuable only if friends are people of good character. "The good path to which a person should cleave [is]…a good friend" (Pirkei Avot 2:13). But who is a good friend? To help answer the question, the Talmud tells the story of Rabbi Yoḥanan, who cleaved to his friend and *hevruta* partner Reish Lakish, and who was inconsolable when Reish Lakish died.

> Rabbi Yoḥanan's students wanted to comfort him, so they invited Rabbi Eleazar ben Pedat to become their teacher's new *hevruta* partner. Honored, the brilliant new partner found a teaching to support every statement Rabbi Yoḥanan made. Yet Rabbi Yoḥanan's despair grew.
>
> "I do not need someone to prove that I am right," he said. "When I studied with Reish Lakish, for every statement I made he would object with twenty-four objections, and I would solve the objections with twenty-four solutions. In that way our understanding of Torah grew, and we enriched the tradition and community" (Bava M'tzia 84a).

- What does the story teach about Rabbi Yoḥanan's character and *dibuk haveirim*?
- Why might love and loyalty sometimes require us to respectfully disagree with our friends?
- Why might Rabbi Eleazar ben Pedat have been so eager to agree with his new *hevruta* partner?
- What advice would you offer to help him become a better friend and study partner?
- How might that apply to you and your *hevruta* partners?

Other traits of a good friend have already been mentioned, including generosity, kindness, honesty and compassion. What qualities do you look for in friends? Which of those qualities make people not only good friends but also strong members of a *kehillah kedoshah?* Why?

Be a Friend to Yourself

If you want to become a better friend to others, start by being a good friend to yourself. Not only will you develop the traits that attract and keep friends, but you will also gain self-respect.

Here are a few tips based on how a good friend would treat you:

1. **Be kind and compassionate.** Pay attention when you feel lonely or hurt and consider how you can be your own best friend. Perhaps you can say something kind or caring to yourself or take yourself out for a walk. Perhaps you can encourage yourself to call someone and get support.

2. **Acknowledge your strengths *and* your weaknesses.** Do not dismiss or exaggerate either. Even as you work on new skills, take pride in those you already have; and as you strive to address your shortcomings, be patient and supportive, like any good friend.

3. **Watch your words.** We all have conversations in our heads. Some are crucial to our well-being—for example, when they encourage us to persist in working through challenges. Other conversations are hurtful and should be stopped, such as those that undermine our self-confidence and good judgment.

4. **Listen to yourself.** Do you speak respectfully to yourself, or do you use unkind, impatient language? Do your words encourage and inspire you or discourage you and fuel your anger, self-pity or negativity? Remember: How you speak to yourself can influence both how you feel and how you behave.

EXPERIENCE

BEST FRIEND, FRIEND, FRIENDLY

You can't be everyone's best friend or even be everyone's friend. But you can be *friendly* with just about everyone. Think about it. Who doesn't deserve a "hello"? How might greeting people by name help you feel good about yourself? How might it make others feel, and how might it strengthen your *kehillah kedoshah*?

Try it. Make a deal with a friend. For one week, greet as many people by name as you can—on the way to school, in class, at sports practice. Then discuss how the experience of being open and friendly made you both feel and how you think it affected others.

ACTIVITY

Sacred Community in Action: Jewish Youth Groups

Sometimes you may need to build a *kehillah kedoshah* from scratch. But other times you can walk into a ready-made situation. That's the strength of Jewish youth groups. In one place at one time you can meet a bunch of kids your age who share a lot of your values and interests but who are different enough to make the friendships interesting and fun.

Jewish youth groups, including North American Federation of Temple Youth (NFTY, Reform), United Synagogue Youth (USY, Conservative), No'ar Hadash (Reconstructionist) and B'nai B'rith Youth Organization (BBYO, nondenominational) are among the leading youth movements. They are national organizations that have local chapters, weekend retreats and summer camps.

Besides being places to enjoy fun activities, discover new friends and develop leadership skills, youth movements build sacred community through social action projects, such as collecting toys and food for those in need.

Different youth movements sometimes work together as one large community. For example, the Coalition of Jewish Teen Leaders, which includes the presidents of USY, NFTY and BBYO, teamed up to fight bullying and homophobia.

- How might you benefit by joining a Jewish youth group? (If you are already a member, consider what the benefit would be to becoming more active.)

  _____

  _____

  _____

  _____

- What do you or could you contribute to the community at a Jewish youth group?

  _____

  _____

  _____

  _____

EXPERiENCE YOUR SACRED COMMUNiTY iN ACTiON

Choose one activity.

FAMILY TRAITS

No family can be perfect, but every family can improve its relationships. Share with your family the top ten character traits your class created. Discuss which traits make for strong family members, and add other traits you all value. In this way you can create the top ten traits your family members want to strengthen within themselves.

As a reminder of the traits that your family values and commits to, work together to create a piece of art—e.g., a quilt or piece of computer art—that incorporates those traits, and display it in your home.

Stella is:
1. Brave
2. Funny
3. Loyal

WHY WE VALUE YOU

Give every classmate one sheet of paper for each member of the class. Ask them to follow these directions: At the top of each sheet, write the name of one classmate and list three character traits or abilities the person has that you value. On the sheet with your name, write what you value about yourself. (For greater anonymity, you can do this activity on a computer.)

Your teacher will collect the papers, group them by student, then give each group to the student who is named. Enjoy learning what others value about you!

ENLARGE YOUR CIRCLE OF FRIENDS

Joining a youth group can multiply your life's fun factor and enlarge your circle of friends. Explore the youth group opportunities through your synagogue or JCC. If you are not a member, join! If you are a member, become more active!

Respect
Kavod כָּבוֹד

What do you do when you think a rule is unfair? Do you grumble? Speak up? Discuss it with your friends? Go viral with an outraged tweet?

It May Be the Law, but Is It Fair?

Imagine the following scenario: You are one of several sisters. Your community has just passed a law denying women the rights of inheritance. Your uncles—not you—will inherit your parents' property.

Working in a small group, develop an action plan to protect your rights. After all the groups have presented their plans to the class, discuss which plan would be most effective and fair, and why.

In ancient times it was common to deny women the right to inherit property. The Torah tells the story of how five Israelite sisters responded to such a law, which prohibited them from inheriting their father's share of property in the land of Israel. Here's what happened.

The daughters of Zelophehad—Mahlah, Noah, Hoglah, Milcah and Tirtzah—came forward. They stood at the entrance of the Tent of Meeting before Moses, Eleazer the priest, the leaders and the whole community and declared: "Our father died in the wilderness. He was not part of Korah's clique, which banded together against The Eternal.

"He died without leaving a son. Let our father's name not be lost to his family because he did not have a son. Give us a share of property as an inheritance in the land of Israel amidst our father's kin."

Moses brought their case before the presence of The Eternal. And God said to Moses, "The daughters' plea is just. Give them a hereditary share in the land of Israel amidst their father's kin. Furthermore, speak to the Israelite people, saying, 'If a man dies without leaving a son, you shall transfer his property to his daughter'" (Numbers 27:1–8).

EXPERiENCE

LET'S TALK ABOUT IT: NUMBERS 27:1–8

Working with a *hevruta* partner or small group, reread the text from Numbers. Take turns reading aloud. Note that the Torah does not credit one sister as the speaker. Instead, it says that the daughters of Zelophehad came forward and spoke, suggesting that they spoke as one.

Do you think the sisters were in total agreement about what to say from the start? Why or why not? If several sisters had wanted to use more aggressive or hostile words, what might the other sisters have said to persuade them not to? Do you think that was wise or timid? Why?

Working in a small group, create *midrash* by role-playing the different points of view until all the sisters come to an agreement or compromise about the words and tone of voice they will use. Be prepared to discuss with your class the experience of compromising and choosing an appropriate tone of voice.

ACTIVITY

Making Sacred Meaning

Study the text below with a partner. Go over it with your class.

The sage Ben Zoma taught:

Who is shown respect—the person who shows respect for others. As it is said, "For those who show *kavod* for me Me [God], I will show *kavod*" (*Pirkei Avot* 4:1).

Why do you think Ben Zoma compared showing respect for people to God's response to being shown respect?

_____

_____

_____

_____

_____

_____

_____

_____

A Double-Voltage Strategy: Self-Respect and Respect for Others

Not only did the sisters win justice for themselves, but they also helped change Jewish law to protect other women. *How did they do it?*

For starters, they showed respect, or *kavod*—not only for themselves, but also for those they disagreed with. They spoke up; they did not lash out. They sought justice, not revenge. They may have felt hurt, disrespected or even betrayed, but they followed a path of *kavod* and courtesy, or *derekh eretz*.

The payoff? Their efforts to gain justice stayed on track. No one was distracted by bad behavior, self-righteousness or disrespectful speech. No one had to defend him- or herself against angry charges and accusations. Everyone remained cool-headed and focused on finding a just and respectful solution to the problem.

How Do You Show Respect?

The sage Hillel offered a basic rule of good behavior that uses self-respect as a guide to showing respect for others: "What is hateful to you, do not do to others…" (*Shabbat* 31a). In other words, don't do to others what you don't want them to do to you. Consider if, before speaking or taking an action, it would be helpful to ask yourself, "How would I feel if someone treated me like that?"

Filling in Details of the Rule

Building on what Hillel said, Rabbi Akiva taught, "What is hateful to you, do not do to others; therefore, do not hurt others; do not speak ill of them; do not reveal their secrets; let their honor and property be as dear to you as your own" (*Avot de Rabbi Natan*).

EXPERiENCE

HOW I WANT TO BE TREATED

In addition to a list of "don'ts," you also may have a list of "dos" for how you want to be treated. For example, you may want others to be considerate of your feelings and forgiving of your mistakes.

Create a list of seven ways you want to be treated.

1. _____
2. _____
3. _____
4. _____
5. _____
6. _____
7. _____

Consulting your list, work with classmates to develop ten to fifteen guidelines for how to treat one another. Decide which of the final rules also apply to how you should treat your teachers and family members.

If there is time, create a poster for your class, school or home to remind you of the guidelines and to help you share them with others.

You can respectfully disagree with others—including your teachers, parents and friends—if you are polite. This means listening patiently and using the same respectful language and tone you want others to use with you.

ACTIVITY

Sacred Community in Action: Bet Tzedek Legal Services

If Bet Tzedek Legal Services had been around in ancient times, the daughters of Zelophe<u>h</u>ad could have turned to it for help. What led Stanly Levy and his colleague, Luis Lainer, to create Bet Tzedek in Los Angeles in 1974? They were outraged that poor people had inadequate access to legal assistance. They refused to ignore the injustice suffered by Holocaust survivors and other seniors who lacked the means to fight evictions and consumer fraud, or to obtain government benefits that were due them.

So Levy brought together a group of eighteen friends—lawyers, law students, legal secretaries and social workers—each of whom donated five dollars a month to rent a storefront office and volunteered one night a month to help low-income people with their legal problems.

They succeeded beyond their wildest dreams. Today thousands of lawyers volunteer their time, talent and expertise through Bet Tzedek, helping fifteen thousand people a year with their legal problems, ranging from employee rights to caregiver issues.

Deuteronomy 16:20 commands, "Justice, justice pursue" and *Bet Tzedek* means "House of Justice." What is the relationship between pursuing justice for the elderly and needy and showing respect for them?

_____

_____

How might you pursue justice to show your self-respect? _____

_____

_____

How might you pursue justice to show respect for others? _____

_____

_____

Bullying is the opposite of respectful behavior. It is rude, mean-spirited and sometimes violent. It can be verbal, like teasing or name-calling; physical, like hitting or forcing a person to do something against his or her will; or it can be indirect, like shunning someone or spreading vicious rumors or lies.

There is *never* justification for bullying. If you or someone you know becomes the target of a bully, demand that the bully stop. Alternatively, seek help. For example, speak to a trusted adult, like a parent, rabbi or school official, or go to a safe site such as *www.stopbullying.gov*.

But suppose you feel tempted to bully someone—perhaps a younger sibling or someone who's not your friend. Then remember that *feeling* tempted is no sin. It's part of being human. Taking action—well, that's another story.

Pirkei Avot 4:1 teaches, "Who is strong? The person who controls the impulse to do wrong." Although it's human to be tempted, strong people struggle to overcome their hurtful and destructive impulses. In short, Judaism teaches that it is the bully—not the victim—who is the weakling.

EXPERiENCE
ON THE FRINGE

As a sign of your commitment to treating yourself and others with respect and to making your school bully-free, consider designing a macramé bracelet that you and your classmates can wear. (Internet sites offer free instructions—just search "instructions macramé bracelets".) The strings that you weave together can symbolize the diverse people in your *kehillah kedoshah.*

As an alternative, you can make the fringe, or tassel, of a *tallit* (prayer shawl), which you can attach to a key ring or necklace. The fringe is called *tzitzit.* (Instructions are available on the Internet—search "instructions tying tzitzit".) You may even want to develop a fundraising project by producing *tzitzit* on a key ring to sell at your school and synagogue. You can contribute the profits to an organization that fights intolerance and promotes respect for others.

Finally, just as we recite a blessing before putting on a *tallit,* before putting on your bracelet or *tzitzit* you may want to recite Ben Zoma's words or write a blessing that expresses your gratitude for the gift of sacred community.

Respecting Other People's Stuff

Here's how our ancient sage Rabbi Joshua ben Hananiah learned the value of showing respect for other people's property.

One day, while walking in the broiling hot sun, Rabbi Joshua ben Hananiah noticed a path other travelers had made through the field before him. Without thinking, he took the shortcut to save time. On seeing him, a girl called out, "Rabbi, are you not trespassing?"

"No, for other travelers made this path, not I," replied the rabbi.

"Exactly! It was trespassers like you who beat a path through our field." *(Eruvin 53b)*

The girl taught the rabbi that there is no excuse for disrespecting someone's property. (This includes no justification for damaging or destroying other people's stuff because they did it to yours.)

Here are four guidelines to help you treat other people's property with respect:

1. Ask before borrowing. Do not take anything without receiving permission from the person who owns or is responsible for the item.

2. Take care of what you borrow. Treat borrowed property as if it were your own, or more precious than your own.

3. If you damage or lose a borrowed item, immediately take responsibility by apologizing and repairing or replacing it.

4. Don't borrow what you can't afford to replace.

EXPERiENCE

COMMUNAL SING DOWN

It's time for a sing down! Form two teams. Give each team ten minutes to write a list of songs that mention or are about community (e.g., "We Are the World" and "This Land Is Your Land") or mention or are about an individual (e.g., "I've Got to Be Me" and "Oh, My Darling Clementine"). When the time is up, have the teams alternate singing a few lines from each song on their lists. The team with the most songs wins. (A song may be disqualified if a majority of the class votes it down because its lyrics are disrespectful or not on topic. Teachers can be tie-breakers.)

Respect for privacy is not only about what we see. It is also about what we say…or *don't* say. So the Book of Proverbs teaches, "A gossip gives away secrets, but a loyal soul keeps a confidence" (Proverbs 11:13). In fact, we often value friends and family because we can share our private thoughts and feelings with them without fear of betrayal.

But is sharing a confidence always disloyal, or are there times when it is a *mitzvah* and a sign of concern and respect? For example, if we know someone is hurting him- or herself or plans to hurt others, not only may we be *obligated* to tell someone else, but it also may be the best way to show our loyal support.

Here are several questions to consider when deciding if it is appropriate to share private information and whom to share it with.

1. Is the person at serious risk and/or creating a threat to others?

2. What harm might I cause by telling? By *not* telling?

3. Will it be better to talk with the person or to a trusted adult, such as a parent, teacher or rabbi?

4. Can I limit how much I reveal and still protect those at risk?

EXPERIENCE YOUR SACRED COMMUNITY IN ACTION

Choose one activity.

SETTING FAMILY & PERSONAL GOALS

With your family, create a list of five actions that can help you treat each other with respect and five actions that can strengthen your self-respect. For example, you might describe how you will listen and speak to one another when you disagree and what you will do to take better care of your body and personal property.

After you create the list, post it in a family room, like the kitchen or playroom, and meet regularly to discuss the family's progress in reaching its goals.

IT'S ALL WRITE TO BE SKIT-ISH

With your classmates, write a skit that teaches young children how to show respect to one another and to adults. Practice and then perform the skit for younger classes.

RESPECTING THE WORLD AROUND YOU

Volunteer at a local charitable organization as a way to show concern and respect for others. For example, you and your family might join a program to distribute food or clothes to those in need. Helping to provide these basics is not only respectful but also a way to pursue justice, or *tzedek*.

Responsibility

Ah'rayut אַחֲרָיוּת

Responsibility is weird. One minute it's a source of pride. *Yup! I'm in charge.* The next it can be a burden. *Ugh! Why me?* When we're feeling the "ugh" more than the "yup," we may expect others to cut us some slack even if we haven't been so easy on them. Think about it. How much slack do you cut your mom or dad, your teachers, friends or siblings? Do you hold yourself as accountable as you hold others? Why or why not?

EXPERiENCE

AN INVENTORY OF RESPONSIBILITIES

Working with a peer, interview each other to explore the differences in your experience and views on responsibility. Here are some questions to get you started.

1. What, if any, chores do you have at home? How committed are you to doing them?

2. What responsibilities do you have as a student? Which are priorities for you? Why? How well do you meet those responsibilities?

3. Do you play, or have you ever played, a team sport? If yes, what did/do your coach and teammates expect of you? What did/do you expect of them (for example, that they arrive on time)?

4. Do you receive an allowance? If yes, what expenses is it intended to cover? Are you expected to save a portion? Do you?

5. Have you ever worked, for example, as a volunteer or babysitter? If yes, describe your responsibilities. What were your supervisor's responsibilities to you (for example, to give you clear instructions and training)? How did it work out?

6. What is the most responsible action you have ever taken? What were the benefits? What is the least responsible? What were the consequences?

7. Do you think you are a responsible young adult? Why or why not?

8. What has helped you most to become responsible? Why?

9. Who is a strong peer role model for you as a responsible person? Why?

10. What new responsibility do you look forward to taking on next year? Why?

After completing your interviews, compare and contrast your experiences. What, if anything, surprised you? Consider discussing some of your findings with the class. Find out if there are responsibilities that most of you have and what you think their value is.

Why Fuss about Responsibility?

People depend on one another to be responsible. Irresponsible behavior not only may be disappointing, it also may be unsafe. Would you hire a careless engineer to build a skyscraper, or firefighters who respond to 911 only when they're in the mood? Has someone's irresponsibility ever put you in harm's way? If yes, what happened, and how did you feel? Has your own failure to act responsibly ever caused a problem? Do you think others were justified in being upset? Why or why not?

No one becomes a responsible person overnight. It takes years of physical, mental and emotional growth, experience and a lot of perseverance. Along the way we stumble and make mistakes of every sort—we're late, we forget, we lose stuff and we break a few promises and rules.

It's all part of the learning curve that creates a responsible life. Fortunately, no one expects us to be perfect. But we are asked to take responsibility for what we do—or don't do—and work on improving. In fact, that's a major theme of the Bible, starting with Adam and Eve.

When Adam and Eve disobeyed God by eating the forbidden fruit from the tree of knowledge of good and evil, instead of taking responsibility for their actions, they tried to hide. Of course, that was futile, but Genesis tells us that God played along, calling out:

> "Where are you?… Did you eat from the tree from which I had forbidden you to eat?"

> The man said, "The woman whom You put at my side gave me from the tree, and so I ate."

> Then the Eternal said to the woman, "What is this you have done?"

> The woman said, "The serpent tempted me, and I ate." (Genesis 3:9, 11–13)

EXPERiENCE

LET'S TALK ABOUT IT: GENESIS 3:9, 11–13

Working with a *hevruta* partner, reread the text from Genesis. Take turns reading aloud. Discuss why you think the text is worded "God *said* to the woman, 'What is this you have done?'" rather than "God *asked*."

How might Adam and Eve's reactions be compared to those of little children who have made a mistake? How might the rest of the story, in which Adam and Eve leave home (Eden) and need to work for their food, be compared to the responsibilities you will have one day? Do you think God was punishing them or helping them to grow up? Why?

In the tradition of filling in missing information by creating *midrash,* develop a one-act play with your partner in which Adam and Eve prepare to leave Eden and discuss what their lives will be like in the future. Consider if and how their relationship with God and with each other might change. If there is time, you can perform your play for the class.

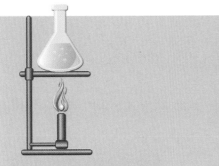

EXPERiENCE

DECISION DILEMMA

Working with a partner, use the four steps to making a responsible decision (see text on the right) to decide what you would do in the following situation. You need a new bike helmet and see one on sale for only one day for $30. You have the exact amount of money but owe a friend $12, which you promised to pay back tomorrow. (Your parents will not permit you to withdraw money from your savings account.) What do you do? Be sure to list your priorities and brainstorm possible solutions.

When everyone is ready, come together as a class and share the priorities you listed, the options you brainstormed and your final decision. Vote on the decision that seems most responsible and practical. Be prepared to explain why you cast your vote as you did.

Four Steps to Making a Responsible Decision

Chocolate or strawberry ice cream? Hooded or crew sweatshirt? You may stop for a moment to consider your preference, but such decisions don't have a major impact on you or anyone else. Other decisions, however, matter a great deal, like whether you should study for your math test or show up for baseball practice.

The following steps can help you make thoughtful, responsible decisions either by yourself or with the help of an adult or friend.

1. Clearly state your issue or dilemma.
2. List your priorities and options. (Brainstorm creative options.)
3. Weigh the benefits and consequences of each choice based on your priorities.
4. Make your decision.

Once you have made your decision and taken action (or not), it is helpful to evaluate and learn from the results. Did your choice help anyone or improve a situation? Are you satisfied, or would you make a different decision next time?

Becoming a Bar or Bat Mitzvah

As we grow older and mature, the secular community grants us the legal rights and responsibilities of adult citizens. They include the right to vote, to apply for a driver's license and to serve in the armed forces and the responsibility to abide by the laws of the land.

Jewish law also grants rights and responsibilities to us as adult members of the community. We automatically receive them when we become a bar or bat mitzvah at thirteen (or, in some communities, girls receive them at twelve). They include the right to be counted in a *minyan* (a quorum of ten Jewish adults), to receive an *aliyah* (honor of being called to the Torah) and to serve as a legal witness. They also include responsibility for performing the *mitzvot*.

Up until the time one becomes a bar or bat mitzvah he or she is expected to study the *mitzvot* and learn to fulfill them, but it is our parents who are held responsible for our actions. When we reach the age of bar or bat mitzvah we take on full responsibility. Some parents acknowledge that shift by reciting this blessing at the bar or bat mitzvah celebration:

(for a boy) .בָּרוּךְ שֶׁפְּטָרַנִי מֵעָנְשׁוֹ שֶׁל זֶה

(for a girl) .בָּרוּךְ שֶׁפְּטָרַנִי מֵעָנְשָׁהּ שֶׁל זוֹ

Blessed is the One who has freed me from responsibility for (the actions of) this child.

ACTIVITY

Why Thirteen?

The tradition of becoming a bar or bat mitzvah is not mentioned in the Torah. (Moses and Queen Esther may have been heroic, but as teens *they* didn't have to chant a *haftarah* or write and deliver a speech.) The first time our sacred texts refer to this life-cycle event is in a commentary by a second-century sage, Judah ben Temah.

He taught that "At five one should study the Bible; at ten one should study Mishnah; at thirteen one is ready to do *mitzvot*…" (*Pirkei Avot* 5:25).

- Do you feel ready to accept responsibility for fulfilling the *mitzvot?* Why or why not?

_____

_____

- If you could choose a different age at which to become a bar or bat mitzvah, what would it be? Why?

_____

_____

- Do you think that taking responsibility for fulfilling the *mitzvot* requires adult Jews to be perfect? Please explain your answer and describe what you think are reasonable expectations and why.

_____

_____

EXPERiENCE

OY! IT'S HEAVY!

The teaching from *Deuteronomy Rabbah* 1:10 (see right side of page) is a commentary on Deuteronomy 1:9. In that verse Moses tells the Israelites:

> "I cannot carry the burden of you myself."

Moses waited to ask for the Israelites' help until he had led them from slavery to freedom and they had received God's teachings at Mount Sinai. Working in a small group, discuss why you think Moses waited until that point and why he ultimately did reach out to the Israelites rather than just pray to God for help. What can Deuteronomy 1:9 teach us about the need to work collaboratively with our leaders?

Brainstorm actions you and your classmates can take to help your teachers, principal, cantor or rabbi create a caring *kehillah kedoshah*. Then collaborate on a mural that illustrates the words of *Deuteronomy Rabbah* 1:10 by drawing from your list of actions.

Taking Responsibility for the Community

Our tradition teaches that "A community is too heavy for anyone to carry alone" *(Deuteronomy Rabbah 1:10)*. Therefore, we are expected not only to care for our own needs and the needs of our family, but also to contribute to the welfare of our community.

$\mathcal{S}$ometimes our responsibility to the community requires us to pick up litter and recycle trash. Other times it guides us to volunteer in hospitals or old-age homes. And yet other times it asks us to help those suffering from famine or war.

To fulfill such responsibilities we must be able to see beyond ourselves, beyond our own needs and desires. As the following tale teaches, that isn't always easy.

There once was a wealthy miser who refused to help the poor. He had lived in his village for more than forty years, yet he had never contributed so much as a copper coin to the public welfare. One day while visiting him the rabbi asked, "Whom do you see when you look out your window?"

"I see the ragged peddler Isaac selling used clothes to the widow Lieb," responded the miser.

"And whom do you see when you look in your mirror?" the rabbi asked.

The miser laughed and said, "Myself, of course."

"Of course," repeated the rabbi. "Both the window and the mirror are made of glass, but the mirror's silver backing blocks your view of others. Similarly, your love of silver is blocking your soul's view of the world."

How could the miser unblock his soul? What suggestions do you have to help him live as a responsible, caring member of the community? Would it be necessary or desirable for him to give away all his wealth to the poor? Why or why not?

Our Responsibility to Rebuke

The story of the miser and the rabbi tells how the rabbi gently explained the error of the miser's ways. By doing so the rabbi performed the *mitzvah* of rebuke, or *tokheihah*, and increased the likelihood of the miser becoming a better person.

Tokheihah teaches that it is our responsibility to speak up when someone behaves in a selfish or hurtful way. For example, we are asked to reprimand a person who is careless or violent on the playing field or at school.

Activity continued on page 42

Activity continued from page 41

Our sage Maimonides instructed us to follow these three guidelines when performing the *mitzvah* of *tokhei<u>h</u>ah*:

1. Be guided by the desire to help the wrongdoer.

2. Deliver the reprimand in privacy, free from public embarrassment.

3. Speak to the wrongdoer with compassion.

Which of the three guidelines is most challenging to you? Why? How might you overcome the challenge?

_____

_____

EXPERiENCE

A SCAVENGER HUNT WITH A BONUS

Divide your class into two teams. Using your eyes and the vision of your soul, search your synagogue, school and/or the synagogue's website to locate opportunities to help the community. Each team will have thirty minutes to search and make a list of every opportunity. For example, you might see a sign asking for donations to a winter coat drive or a fence that needs fresh paint.

Each item on a team's list will receive one point. The team with the most points wins. However, both teams will have two weeks to participate in the opportunities. For every one a student participates in, his or her team will receive five bonus points. (The opportunity can be on either of the two lists.)

At the end of two weeks the bonus points will be added to each team's total, and either a new winner will be declared or the winning team will remain standing!

According to Jewish law, our responsibility increases the longer we are part of a community.

> "When a person lives in a town for thirty days, that person becomes obligated to contribute to the soup kitchen; for three months to donate to the *tzedakah* fund; for six months to the clothing fund; for nine months to the burial fund; and twelve months for the repair of the town walls" (*Bava Batra* 8a).

The more time, concern, effort and *tzedakah* we invest in our community, the greater the satisfaction in knowing that we have helped it grow and thrive. Being responsible isn't just the right thing to do; it is also the rewarding way to live.

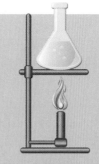

EXPERiENCE

GROWING RESPONSIBILITY

Working with a partner or small group, discuss why you think the requirement to take on increased responsibility the longer we are part of a community is fair or unfair. Should there be age limits or exceptions? Why?

Consider how Jewish laws regarding increased responsibility might relate to your school. What responsibilities can students take on (for example, sending cards to ailing students, beautifying the hallways or ushering at Shabbat prayer services)?

Make a list of increasing responsibilities for students in grades five to seven. Be prepared to present it to the class with an explanation of how the actions would strengthen the individuals and the community.

ACTIVITY

Sacred Community in Action: Hazon

hazon

JEWISH INSPIRATION. SUSTAINABLE COMMUNITIES.

The first chapter of Genesis, or *Bereishit,* teaches that humans were created as God's partners in caring for Creation. "They shall be guardians over the fish of the sea, the birds of the sky, the cattle, the entire earth and all the creeping things that creep on the earth" (Genesis 1:26).

Hazon, which means "vision" in Hebrew, is an organization that helps Jews live as responsible members of the community and guardians of the earth. Through its Community Supported Agriculture (CSA) network in North America and Israel Hazon makes healthful foods more available, supports sustainable farming practices (such as organic farming methods) and reduces the use of fossil fuels for transporting food. Hazon also helps the Jewish community minimize its carbon footprint by sponsoring bike-riding activities in North America and Israel.

Hazon's Jewish Farm School practices sustainable agriculture. Its education and farming programs are based on the Jewish "traditions of using food as a tool for social justice and spiritual mindfulness." These traditions include giving all people access to good nutrition, treating animals and the earth with respect and reciting prayers of thanks for life's goodness and the earth's bounty.

• Based on the information above, what do you think Hazon's vision of a *kehillah kedoshah* is?

_____

_____

_____

• How might Hazon's programs help you live as a responsible member of the community and a guardian of the earth? (Before answering, you may want to visit www.hazon.org.)

_____

_____

_____

EXPERiENCE YOUR SACRED COMMUNiTY iN ACTiON

Choose one activity.

GET INVOLVED

Share what you have learned about responsibility increasing as one is part of a community for a longer time. Discuss how your family may want to take on new responsibilities—for example, by volunteering in the synagogue or with another local organization or by participating in a Hazon program.

WHO CARRIES THE BURDEN OF RESPONSIBILITY?

Do you have any idea how many people it takes to responsibly run a synagogue and school? Working with your teacher or another member of your school staff, make a list of all the people who work for the synagogue and school, along with the many volunteers who help keep things going.

Of course, you will list the rabbi, cantor, principal and teaching staff. But don't forget the people who head up committees, empty trash or shovel the snow in the winter. Remember all the folks who usher at services, put away prayerbooks after services and organize food drives and carpools.

Consider how you or your class might express appreciation for all those people.

Social Justice

Tikkun Olam תִּקּוּן עוֹלָם

EXPERiENCE

JEWISH LEADER WANTED

Working in small groups, discuss the story of Noah and brainstorm reasons why Noah wasn't chosen as a patriarch despite being just and following God's commands.

Consider what someone worthy of being a patriarch or matriarch might have done differently and brainstorm the qualities of that person. Then write a job posting for "Leader of the Jews." Describe the character and type of role model that is required.

Be prepared to share your job posting with the class. Ask who would be interested in applying for the job and why or why not. If you have a taker, conduct a job interview!

Blind obedience is not what God desires. In fact, our sacred texts teach that God often hopes for pushback. Take, for example, the story of Noah.

The Bible says that "Noah was a just man…Noah walked with God" (Genesis 6:9). Then it describes the out-of-control human corruption in the world, God's plan to send a great flood and God's instructions to Noah for building a *ginormous* ark to save himself, his family and a multitude of animals.

Noah obeyed *every* detail. The Bible emphasizes that, stating it four times:

"Noah did…as God **commanded** him" (Genesis 6:22).

"Noah did just as The Eternal **commanded** him" (Genesis 7:5).

"…[The male and female animals] came to Noah into the ark, as God had **commanded** Noah" (Genesis 7:9).

"…[The animals entered the ark] as God had **commanded** him [Noah]" (Genesis 7:16).

Yet despite fulfilling God's every command, Noah isn't our patriarch; he didn't make the cut.

Noah's flaw was his indifference to evil and suffering in the world. He silently watched his neighbors head straight for disaster, neither urging them to change their ways nor pleading for God's mercy.

It's true that people often need to follow orders strictly, as Noah did. In fact, when one serves in the military, national security may depend on it. But serving God requires more than simply obeying commands.

Serving God requires us to confront wrongdoing and seek justice. That is why we perform acts of social justice, or *tikkun olam*—literally, "repair of the world." Sometimes *tikkun olam* means feeding the hungry or sheltering the homeless. Other times it means bringing peace or comfort to the victims of war or natural disaster. And yet other times it means protecting the innocent from God's wrath.

ACTIVITY

The Sacred Act of Pushing Back

This ancient *midrash* helps explain why Noah didn't measure up.

Noah stepped out of the ark and surveyed the havoc and destruction caused by the flood. "Master of the universe!" he cried out. "You are called the Merciful One. You should have shown mercy for your creatures."

God answered, "Before the flood I lingered at your side, speaking with you so that you could ask for mercy for the world. But the moment you heard that you would be safe in the ark, nothing else touched your heart…. Only now that the world has been destroyed do you speak up." (Zohar: The Book of Enlightenment)

Enter Abraham

The Bible tells us that—generations after the great flood—God threatened to destroy the evil cities of Sodom and Gomorrah. Abraham stood on the outskirts of Sodom, knowing God's intention and free to walk away. It was not his town; why would it be his business? Yet our patriarch came forward, seeking justice from God, saying:

"Will You wipe out the innocent along with the guilty? Perhaps there are fifty innocent people in the city. Will you sweep away the place and not forgive it for the sake of the innocent fifty within its midst? Heaven forbid that You would do such a thing, to bring death upon the innocent along with the guilty…. Shall the Judge of all the earth not do what is just?" (Genesis 18:23–25)

The Bible continues with God agreeing to save Sodom if fifty innocent people can be found. Emboldened, Abraham shaves off five. God okays forty-five, but Abraham goes down to forty. Negotiations move along until God agrees to save the city if ten innocent people can be found.

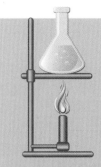

EXPERiENCE

LET'S TALK ABOUT IT:
GENESIS 18:23–25

Working with a *hevruta* partner, reread the text from Genesis. Take turns reading aloud.

Compare and contrast the Bible story and *midrash* about Noah with the story of Abraham. Which relationship is more inspiring—the one between Noah and God or the one between Abraham and God? Why?

The *Amidah* prayer calls God "the shield of Abraham," *Magen Avraham.* How might Abraham's pursuit of justice have made him a shield of God? How might we be such shields when we perform acts of *tikkun olam?*

Create a visual *midrash* by designing a shield of Justice, or *magen Mishpat,* for, as our tradition teaches, "The Eternal is God of Justice" (Isaiah 30:18). Before beginning, consider the words and/or images you want to include. Be prepared to share your design with the class and to explain its connection to *tikkun olam.*

ACTIVITY

Unbelievingly Valuable!

Not only does our tradition urge us to question and even challenge God, it also teaches that at times we must act as if God does not exist.

Rabbi Moshe Leiv of Sassov, who taught that all of Creation serves a sacred purpose, was once asked by a student, "What sacred purpose is served by those who do not believe in God?"

The rabbi smiled and answered, "Such people will never wait for God to help those in need. They teach us to act as if God does not exist and we alone are responsible for the welfare of the world."

Some people think that God is the source of our desire to perform acts of *tikkun olam.* What do you think? Why?

_____

_____

_____

_____

The Prophet Motive

Abraham was both our first patriarch and our first prophet—messenger from God—teaching our people to live with sacred purpose. Moses was the greatest of the prophets, for we received the Torah through him.

We learn about the other prophets from the section of the Bible called the Prophets, or *Nevi'im*. (The three sections of the Bible are Torah, Prophets and Writings, or *Ketuvim*.) Elijah taught us to hold political leaders accountable for their actions. Other prophets, like Amos, Isaiah, Jeremiah and Micah, were among the world's first social activists, advocating for the poor and vulnerable and urging us to pursue *tzedek* and *shalom,* or peace.

EXPERiENCE

WHAT WOULD THE PROPHETS DO?

Jewish tradition teaches that many of our biblical leaders were chosen because they showed concern for God's creatures. We saw Abraham's concern for the innocent of Sodom, and an ancient *midrash* teaches that God chose Moses, a shepherd, to lead the Israelites because of his compassion for the most vulnerable in his flock.

Working with a partner or small group, identify a current event that is of concern to you, such as a war, natural disaster or social or political injustice. (You may search online sources, newspapers, magazines or other media.) Collaborate on writing a dialogue between yourselves and God that expresses your concerns and why they are important, and that states God's point of view. Work with God to brainstorm acts of *tikkun olam* that you can take to help those who suffer.

Be prepared to perform your dialogue for the class and to discuss how the actions you brainstormed could help repair the world. Consider taking one of the actions with others.

ACTIVITY

Making Sacred Meaning

The prophets taught our ancestors how to live as a *kehillah kedoshah,* and their words still speak to us today. Before reading the quotes below, please respond to the following three items.

1. Describe what you think it means to be a religious Jew. _____
   _____
   _____

2. On a scale of 1 to 5 (with 5 representing the highest value), express the importance of rituals in living as a religious Jew. Why? _____
   _____
   _____

3. On a scale of 1 to 5, express the importance of *tikkun olam* in living as a religious Jew. Why? _____
   _____
   _____

Share with a <u>hevruta</u> partner your reasons for answering as you did. Then take turns reading the quotes below aloud. Discuss whether you think the prophets' messages are *religious* or secular teachings and why you think they do or do not belong in our sacred texts.

Let justice flow like water, righteousness like a mighty stream (Amos 5:24).

Learn to do good; seek justice; help the wronged…free the oppressed, share your bread with the hungry (Isaiah 1:17, 58:6, 7).

[This is] what The Eternal requires of you: be just and love goodness and humbly walk with your God (Micah 6:8).

Write your conclusion and reasons regarding why the above teachings do or don't belong in our sacred texts.

_____
_____
_____

Be prepared to share your ideas with your class.

The prophets' message continues to inspire modern religious leaders like Rabbi Harold Kushner. Rabbi Kushner says that when Judaism is "done right" it not only can make life satisfying but, more importantly, also helps fulfill Judaism's ultimate purpose: to transform Creation "into the kind of world that God had in mind when [God] created it."

As Rabbi Tarfon said, "The day is short and the work is great…" (*Pirkei Avot 2:20*). So we start with the sacred community we have and perform one act of *tikkun olam* at a time. What are the benefits of sharing responsibility for such actions with your classmates and synagogue community? What might be the challenges?

EXPERiENCE

WHAT DID GOD HAVE IN MIND?

Reread these quotes from the prophets.

> Let justice flow like water, righteousness like a mighty stream (Amos 5:24).

> Learn to do good; seek justice; help the wronged…free the oppressed, share your bread with the hungry (Isaiah 1:17, 58:6, 7).

> [This is] what The Eternal requires of you: be just and love goodness and humbly walk with your God (Micah 6:8).

Write a paragraph describing the kind of world you think "God had in mind" at the time of Creation. You needn't limit yourself to the ideas expressed by the prophets.

When you have completed your paragraph, work in small groups to compare your ideas. Then write a group vision of how the world was created to be. Be prepared to share the vision with your class and to discuss at least one act of *tikkun olam* you could do as a class that would help realize the vision.

Sacred Community in Action: Panim Institute

The Panim Institute believes in the power of middle and high school students to help make the world a better place, and it gives them opportunities to do just that. It welcomes students who are affiliated and unaffiliated with denominational youth groups, and its programs offer them fun and exciting activities with other young Jews from diverse backgrounds.

Horizons is a Panim program for students in grades 6, 7 and 8. It offers tours of Washington, DC and local experiences in North America, with an emphasis on Jewish history and social and political activism. The programs invite participants to explore the relationship between Jewish and secular values. For more information, go to www.panim.org.

J-Serve is an annual Panim service day that is open to middle and high school students. Usually held in the spring, it helps Jewish students of all backgrounds across the globe to simultaneously perform acts of *tikkun olam* in their communities. Among those who support J-Serve are NFTY, USY, Young Judea, BBYO Panim Institute, Foundation for Jewish Camps and Jewish Student Unions. To learn more, go to www.jserve.org.

How might you benefit by participating in a social justice program with Jewish teens across the world?

_____

_____

_____

_____

_____

_____

ACTIVITY

We Only Have to Do Our Part

Our tradition asks everyone in the community, including those in need, to do their part to improve the world.

As Rabbi Tarfon taught, "You are not responsible to complete the work, but neither are you free to desist from it" (*Pirkei Avot* 2:21).

• Describe an act of *tikkun olam* that a relative or famous person did to which you want to contribute, or describe something similar that you would like to do and explain why.

_____

_____

_____

• Can it be satisfying to contribute to making the world a better place even though you cannot fully repair it? Why or why not?

_____

_____

_____

What Repair Work Interests You?

*T*ikkun olam is, of course, a community affair. Yet because every community is made up of individuals, it comes down to each person doing his or her part. Given all there is to do, how can you decide what to work on?

Here are some questions to help you figure out the types of *tikkun olam* projects that would be best for you.

1. **How much time do you have available to volunteer?** Do you want a one-shot experience, or do you have the time and interest to make an ongoing commitment? Be realistic about the time you have.

2. **What volunteer experiences have you had?** Make a list of your past volunteer experiences, like helping to organize a food or clothing drive. Note which activities you enjoyed, which you want to do again and which are acts of *tikkun olam*.

3. **Do you have a special cause that you care about?** What issues do you care about most— poverty, children, politics? Choosing an issue that you care about will help keep you motivated.

4. **Do you have special talents?** Do you dance, sing or play a musical instrument? Do you enjoy tutoring or coaching? Using your talents can make the project more fun and rewarding.

5. **Are there professional goals that you want to explore?** *Tikkun olam* projects can give you a taste of certain professions. For example, working with children with special needs might help you explore your interest in education or physical therapy.

6. **Do you prefer to work outdoors or indoors?** For example, do you want to join a walk-a-thon, or would you prefer to work in a soup kitchen?

7. **Will you need transportation to and from your destination?** Can you walk, bike or take a train or bus to your destination, or will you need assistance? If you need assistance, be clear about the dates and times.

EXPERiENCE

A MODERN RIFF ON A SACRED TRADITION

When the Holy Temple was destroyed, our Rabbis and prophets urged our ancestors to be strong and take pleasure in life even as they mourned the loss of the Temple. To acknowledge their grief they kept a patch of wall—about 18" by 18"—unpainted in their homes as a reminder that without the Temple their lives were incomplete.

Similarly, we are asked to enjoy our daily lives and celebrate happy occasions even as we remember the need to repair the world. Working in a small group, brainstorm ideas of what you can make for your home or for your mobile device as a reminder of your commitment to *tikkun olam*. For example, you might create a ringtone that uses the song "*Lo Yisa Goy*," which is based on the prophet Isaiah's vision of peace.

When you are ready, meet as a class and consider if, as an act of solidarity, you all want to create the same reminder.

ACTIVITY

Community Hero: Clara Lemlich (1886–1982)

Clara Lemlich understood that although an individual can do a lot, it takes a community to create revolutionary change. So she created that community by inspiring others with her vision of a better world.

Born in the Ukraine, Lemlich immigrated with her family to the United States at age seventeen and began working in New York City's garment industry two weeks later. Like the other employees (many of whom were Jewish women), she worked eleven-hour days, six days a week, for about $3 a week. Outraged by the injustice, she became a union member and workers' rights activist, writing opinion pieces that demanded improved working conditions.

At a union rally on November 22, 1909, speaking in her native Yiddish, Lemlich protested the intolerable conditions in factories and the union's fear of calling a strike. Her words inspired the thousands who attended to stand up and cheer. Before leaving the rally they took an oath to go on strike the next morning.

Dubbed "The Uprising of the Twenty Thousand" because of the extraordinary number of participants, the strike lasted for more than two months and led to revolutionary gains, including shorter working hours and improved wages.

The oath Lemlich asked the union members to recite included these words in Yiddish: "If I turn traitor to the cause I now pledge, may this hand wither from the arm I now raise." It appears to have been inspired by Psalm 137:5: "If I forget you, O Jerusalem, let my right hand wither..."

Why might Lemlich have chosen to base her secular oath on a sacred Jewish text?

_____

_____

_____

_____

EXPERIENCE YOUR SACRED COMMUNITY IN ACTION

Choose one activity.

FAMILY HISTORY

Research your family's experience with social or political activism. For example, find out if any relatives were union organizers or demonstrated, volunteered or worked professionally for social or political causes, such as the civil rights, antiwar or Soviet Jewry movements. Ask if they have contributed in other ways to such causes or if such movements helped them or other relatives when they needed support. Be prepared to share what you learn with your class.

LOCAL OPPORTUNITIES

Research the possibility of participating in a *tikkun olam* event sponsored by your synagogue, and ask how you can help recruit others. Make a commitment to take part in one of the events with a friend or family member and write a pledge of participation—perhaps something similar to the one written by Clara Lemlich. Be prepared to report back to your class after the event.

WHAT'S WRONG WITH THE WORLD?

Meet as a class and brainstorm responses to the question "What are the ten greatest problems of the world?" Among your responses might be issues like hunger, poverty, war, political oppression and disease. If you come up with more than ten ideas, vote on the top ten.

Choose one problem from the ten and commit to a concrete act of *tikkun olam* that can contribute to easing the problem. Then select a date by when you will take action (the date should be within thirty days). Write a pledge of participation and be prepared to report back to your class after you take action.

Connection

Kesher קֶשֶׁר

Ve Jews aren't what we used to be. In fact, we've changed a lot. Our ancestors lived in the land of Israel, sacrificed animals and never heard of Purim, the Talmud or bagels and lox.

Who we are and what we do have evolved over thousands of years. While committed to Judaism's core beliefs, we adapted to changing times. When ancient Jerusalem was destroyed we were exiled from our land and went from sacrificing animals in the Holy Temple to praying in synagogues. We then created the Talmud as a guide for our new lives, and holidays like Purim to celebrate new joys.

Journeying far from our land, where we spoke Hebrew and Aramaic, we spread out across the globe, creating new communities and languages like Ladino and Yiddish, new literature, music and art. We built homes, synagogues and businesses, played baseball and dreidel, lit

Shabbat candles and marched for civil rights. Along the way we suffered tragic losses and established a modern Jewish state. We also began eating bagels and lox—foods never served at Sinai, yet now sacred to our souls.

Who knows how your generation will adapt our ancient tradition to meet the needs and challenges of your time? Yet like the generations before you, the goal will be to sustain our sacred community and add holiness to the world.

EXPERiENCE

A TRADITION OF CHANGE

Times change, and Judaism adapts. Divide your class into several teams. Each will have fifteen minutes to brainstorm a list of *mitzvot*—for example, sending Rosh ha-Shanah greeting cards, pursuing justice and donating tzedakah—that can be done using one modern technology. You can either assign all the teams the same technology—for example, Twitter—or permit each team to choose one.

The teams will present their lists to the class. The team with the longest list will win. Be prepared to discuss how each mitzvah was performed before the technology was available, how it now can be performed with the technology and the plusses and minuses of each way.

EXPERiENCE

IT'S A SMALL YET DIVERSE JEWISH WORLD

There are about thirteen million Jews in the world, which sounds like a lot until you consider the number of Christians (more than two billion) and Muslims (about 1.5 billion). In comparison, we seem like a few specks of dust. Yet we've had a big impact on the world. The *Tanakh* is revered around the globe and has been translated into hundreds of languages; and despite being less than 1 percent of the world's population, since 1901 Jews have won 20 percent of Nobel prizes.

The vast majority of Jews live in Israel and the United States. Many also live in Canada, Australia and South Africa as well as in Europe and South America. A few generations ago more than one million Jews also lived in Iran, Iraq, Syria, Egypt, Morocco and Yemen. But prejudice against the Jews forced them to flee to Israel and the West.

Working independently or with a partner, research the history and culture of Jews from another country. Have at least one classmate research the modern State of Israel.

Be prepared to share with your class what you have learned. If possible, include photographs, art, music and food from the community. After everyone has presented, discuss with which, if any, communities you feel a *kesher,* and why and how it makes you feel. For example, you may feel a connection with a community because your great-grandparents came from there.

Is It Time to Disconnect?

Despite the many changes in Jewish life, we have maintained a strong connection, or *kesher,* to one another and to the land of Israel, *Eretz Yisrael*. We have continued to identify as one people—the Jewish people, *Am Yisrael*—even as we have become loyal citizens of lands outside Israel, the Diaspora.

But some wonder if it's time to disconnect.

For example, tradition says we're all from one family that began four thousand years ago with Abraham and Sarah. That's a *long* time to maintain family ties. Is it realistic for twenty-first–century Jews in Tel Aviv, Paris, Buenos Aires and New York to feel connected? And if it is, when and how should we stay in touch?

Similarly, the time when our forebears lived in *Eretz Yisrael* is ancient history. Is modern Israel really our homeland? Is it the place we all belong? Or should the Jewish state *and* the Jewish Diaspora thrive and support each other while contributing to the larger world?

There are no easy answers to these questions, and even if there were, it's unlikely that all Jews would agree. Fortunately, Judaism doesn't require us to. It only asks that we wrestle with the questions.

Jewish Sacred Wrestling

ACTIVITY

Facing His Fears

The Torah tells us that Jacob was fearful and anxious before his meeting with Esau and that he prayed for God's protection. Why might he have wanted to meet with Esau despite his fears?

_____

_____

_____

_____

_____

With what issues and questions might Jacob have had to struggle before reuniting with his brother? Why?

_____

_____

_____

_____

_____

_____

Wrestling is a sacred Jewish sport. It started centuries before the Olympics, and to this day Jews are passionate wrestlers. Yet unlike Diamond Dallas Page and Giant Bernard, most of us are not fierce musclemen. We're wrestlers of a different sort.

The Torah teaches that it all began with our patriarch Jacob. According to Genesis, Jacob and his twin brother Esau were intense rivals. Being something of a sneak, Jacob cheated Esau (who was no angel himself) out of his birthright blessing. Enraged, Esau threatened to kill Jacob, who fled Canaan, which is what *Eretz Yisrael* was called back then.

Jacob found refuge in Haran, married and raised a family. After twenty years he journeyed back to Canaan, with a plan to meet and make peace with Esau along the way.

The night before meeting Esau…

Jacob was left alone. And a man wrestled with him until dawn broke. When he saw that he could not overtake him, he wrenched Jacob's hip from its socket…. Then he said, "Let me go, for dawn is breaking."

But [Jacob] answered, "I won't let you go unless you bless me."

The other said, "What is your name?"

He responded, '*Ya'akov.*'

Then he said, "Your name will no longer be *Ya'akov* [meaning "heel" or "sneak"]; instead it will be *Yisrael* [meaning "God-wrestler"], for you have wrestled with beings divine and human, and you have prevailed."

Jacob asked, "Please tell me your name."

But he said, "Why do you ask my name?" And he left him with a farewell blessing.

Jacob named the place *Peniel* [meaning "God's face"] because "I have seen a divine being face to face, yet my life was saved." (Genesis 32:25–31)

EXPERiENCE

LET'S TALK ABOUT IT: GENESIS 32:25–31

Working with a *hevruta* partner, reread the text from Genesis. Take turns reading aloud. Discuss with your partner what you think happened and what the story teaches. Use the questions below to guide your discussion.

1. With whom or what do you think Jacob wrestled—God, an angel, another person or his conscience? Why do you think so?
2. Did Jacob wrestle with an opponent or a partner? Why do you think so?
3. What does the meaning of *Ya'akov* versus *Yisrael* reveal about how our patriarch's character changed as a result of the wrestling match?
4. What do you think Jacob meant when he said he had seen "a divine being face to face, yet my life was saved"? Why do you think so?

Names and naming are important in the Bible, and especially in this story. Jacob receives a new name and names the place where he wrestled. When he says "Please tell me your name," the response is "Why do you ask my name?" Do you think it is because Jacob already knows the name, or because the identity is a secret? Create a *midrash* by having the Wrestler respond. If you choose, have Jacob offer a new name and explain why.

Be prepared to share your thoughts on the story and your *midrash* with your class.

Where Are Your Wounds?

In *Ah, but Your Land Is Beautiful*, a novel about apartheid (racial segregation in South Africa), God asks a man who has just died, "Where are your wounds?" When the man responds that he has none, God asks, "Why? Was there nothing worth fighting for?"

What do you think the author, Alan Paton, wanted to teach?

_____

_____

_____

What do you think Jacob would have said he had fought for?

_____

_____

_____

Although Jacob's wrestling match is a bit mysterious and not easy to figure out, we know it brought him "face to face" with God. One understanding is that Jacob wrestled with questions about his character until he faced the truth. According to this view, the names *Am Yisrael* and *Eretz Yisrael* remind us that as descendants of *Yisrael* we must struggle with sacred texts and questions until we see the truth.

Which religious beliefs, such as belief in God, the value of prayer, or how much *tzedakah* to give, have you questioned and struggled with? Do you think it is wise that Judaism encourages us to question our beliefs? Why or why not?

Get Ready to Wrestle

You're almost ready to wrestle, but don't jump into the ring just yet. Exploring personal connections and long-distance relationships can help you wrestle with questions about ties to our people and homeland. So here's a warm-up event (see "Experience" below).

EXPERiENCE

ATTACHMENTS

Think of a place that played an important part in your life and to which you are still emotionally attached—for example, an old neighborhood or school or camp you left at summer's end. Think about the people and shared experiences you enjoyed.

What did it feel like to belong to that community? Why? How did you feel about leaving? What memories about it do you cherish? Do you think you will forget the people, place and memories? Why or why not? Have you maintained a connection with anyone? If yes, why? What have been the challenges of a long-distance relationship? How did you overcome them?

Using a large piece of paper, create a map or drawing of your favorite parts of the place you left—for example, the schoolyard, auditorium, art room and cafeteria of a former school—and list the names of the people who were important to you.

You can share the map or drawing with your class or a partner. Explain why you still value the community and how the relationships continue to affect your life.

As a class, discuss how our ancestors might have felt when they were driven out of the land of Israel. Why do you think they chose not only to become good citizens of their new countries but also to maintain their *kesher* to our homeland and to Jews in the Diaspora? Why do you think they taught their children to do the same?

$\mathcal{O}$-k-a-y, before you go to the mat, we'll stretch your mind one last time with two reasons why ties to *Am* Yisrael and *Eretz Yisrael* remain important to so many Jews.

- **We all belong to the same family tree.** Jewish genealogy includes all our names on the family tree. Rooted in *Eretz Yisrael*, the tree branches across four thousand years of Jewish history in the land of Israel and the Diaspora.

This means that you are not only a twenty-first-century North American Jew but also a living tribute to the lives of King David, the prophet Deborah, Rashi, Anne Frank, Hank Greenberg and pioneers of the modern Jewish state. You belong to all of them and to our homeland, and they all belong to you. Like the Torah and our history, they are every Jew's sacred inheritance and birthright.

ACTIVITY

All Jews Belong: *Klal Yisrael*

Klal Yisrael is a Jewish ideal. It teaches that we all belong to *Am Yisrael,* and it makes room for our diversity, even our disagreements. It embraces God-loving Jews and non-believing Jews, deli-eating Jews and taco-eating Jews, Jews by birth and Jews by choice, Jews from Reconctructionist, Orthodox, Conservative, Reform, interfaith and unaffiliated homes. Every Jew in the world!

Why might *klal Yisrael* be an ideal that is both a comfort and a challenge?

_____

_____

_____

How might the concept of *klal Yisrael* strengthen your classroom as a *kehillah kedoshah?*_____

_____

_____

_____

- **Our connections add impact to our actions and feed our souls.** Just as our ancestors came together in *Eretz Yisrael* to offer sacrifices in the Holy Temple, *Am Yisrael* comes together not only to pray in synagogue but also to perform acts of *tikkun olam*. The larger the goals, the more we must unite and collaborate as a people.

Our Rabbis teach that all Jews are responsible for one another, *Kol Yisrael areivim zeh la-zeh* (Shevuoth 39a). Decades ago Jews around the world rallied support for the oppressed Jews of the former Soviet Union. Raising millions of dollars, petitioning political leaders and organizing demonstrations, we persisted for years until our people were liberated and resettled in *Eretz Yisrael*. This pursuit of justice was *Am Yisrael* power at its best!

We also pursue *tzedek* in the larger world. When New Orleans, Haiti, Japan and East Africa were devastated by natural disasters, Jewish leaders mobilized Israeli and North American Jews to open their wallets and roll up their sleeves to aid those who suffered. We could have contributed to secular organizations, and many of us did. But contributing as members of *Am Yisrael* added sacred meaning to our actions and nurtured our souls.

You may not always agree with your classmates' views on our people and homeland, but together you can wrestle with the sacred questions they raise and explore new possibilities. If you listen respectfully to the diverse opinions of others, you can grow as individuals and become a stronger sacred community.

Keep in Touch

We're unlikely to develop a meaningful connection to friends or family with whom we're never in touch. That's also true with our extended Jewish family and *Eretz Yisrael*. Here are a few options you and your classmates can explore as you consider the connections you want to build.

1. Learn more about the history and culture of other Jewish communities—their music, literature, art, food and traditions—and share what you learn.

2. Collaborate with other Jewish communities on a social justice project. Your local federation can help you be in touch.

3. Build relationships with Jews in other denominations or other Diaspora communities and Israel. For example, work with your youth movement to meet with Israeli scouts, the *Tzofim,* via Skype.

4. Invite one or several teens to speak with your class about their experience with a summer program in Israel.

5. Attend e-Camp, an international summer camp based in a digital village on Mount Carmel in Israel. It's open to kids ages 8–18. For more information you can contact www.eCamp4u.com.

EXPERiENCE

PLEASE STEP INTO THE RING

Now you are ready. Here are the questions with which you will wrestle: Should your local Jewish community strengthen, maintain or disconnect from its ties to *Am Yisrael* and/or *Eretz Yisrael?* If you think your community should strengthen or maintain its connection, why? What actions can help it strengthen or maintain its ties? If you think it should disconnect, why do you think so, and what might you miss if ties were cut with the larger community and our homeland?

You will need a wrestling partner to ask you the above questions and any follow-up questions he or she has. Instead of physically touching, you will wrestle by going back and forth with the questions and answers. Each time you answer, your partner can ask a new question to help you explore and express your beliefs.

Before wrestling, you and your partner can have planning time and choose wrestling names. You may clear an area—even rope it off like a wrestling ring. Your language must be civil, but you and your partner can "get into each other's face" as long as you don't touch one another. You can move around the ring to get out of each other's way.

A "referee" will announce your wrestling names and time the match. (You will have three minutes.) Class applause will determine who prevailed.

ACTIVITY

Sacred Community in Action: Visiting Israel

The best way to develop a personal *kesher* is to have a personal experience. That is why a trip to Israel is key. Your visit will help you develop a firsthand understanding of and feeling for *Eretz Yisrael* and the modern Jewish state—*Medinat Yisrael*. Whether it raises new questions or offers new answers, it will certainly make you a stronger wrestler in the tradition of *Am Yisrael*.

Contact information is listed below for several teen summer trips to Israel.

- **Reform/NFTY** www.nftyisrael.org
- **Conservative/USY** www.usy.org
- **Reconstructionist/Noar Hadash** www.noarhadash.org
- **Cross-Denominational/Nesiya** www.nesiya.org
- **Young Judaea** www.youngjudaea.org
- **BBYO** www.bbyo.org

For information about other Israel experiences, including summer camps and family trips, contact The Jewish Agency at www.jafi.org or your synagogue.

Describe one place or experience you look forward to in Israel and why.

_____

_____

EXPERIENCE

PLAN A TRIP TO ISRAEL

It's never too early to think about what to do and see when you visit Israel. Planning a trip with your class can help you explore your options and wrestle with questions you have. Whether or not you make the trip together, the process can strengthen you as a community.

Working with a partner or a small group, research the places you want to visit on a four-week trip—for example, the Galilee, Haifa, Tel Aviv, Jerusalem, Beersheva and Eilat. Include the sites and activities each place offers, like swimming with the dolphins in Eilat, seeing a soccer game and open-air market *(shuk)* in Tel Aviv and spending Shabbat in Jerusalem. Also think about the people you want to meet, including Jewish and Arab teens and Jewish immigrants. Make a list of words you want to learn in Hebrew.

When you complete your research, plan the trip with your partner or group and present it to your class using a map to show the route you will take and explaining why you included each place on your trip.

Enjoy your explorations and have fun creating new connections along the way!

EXPERIENCE YOUR SACRED COMMUNITY IN ACTION

Choose one activity.

FAMILY WRESTLING MATCH

Share with your family, perhaps over Shabbat dinner, what you learned about the Jewish tradition of wrestling with questions. Invite your family to raise questions about Judaism or God with which they struggle and consider holding a "wrestling match" after dinner.

JEWISH GENEALOGY

Supplies for class project: butcher paper, colored construction paper, tape, scissors, crayons or pens. Tape together several pieces of butcher paper and draw an outline of a large tree with roots and branches to represent the Jewish people's family tree. Label the base where the roots are *Eretz Yisrael.*

Cut the shape of at least 120 leaves from construction paper. Write your name on one leaf and tape it on a branch labeled "Twenty-first Century." Then brainstorm with your class the names of ten to fifteen biblical ancestors who lived in *Eretz Yisrael* and write the names on leaves that you tape to the roots of the tree.

Use the remaining leaves to write the names of friends, relatives and famous Jews—for example, Rabbis, Nobel prize winners, entertainers, artists and writers—and tape them on branches that are labeled with the appropriate century. The object is to fill as many branches as possible on our family tree with the names of Jews who lived in different places and at different times.

(continue on page 70)

JEWISH MULTI-CULTURAL DESSERT FUNDRAISER

Class project: Research recipes for desserts made in Jewish communities in Israel and the Diaspora. You can search for recipes at home, in your synagogue library and online. Either publish the recipes in booklet form or use them to run a bake sale as a fundraiser. You can donate the profits to a Jewish organization that supports *tikkun olam* projects in Israel or in another part of the world.

Celebration

Simhah שִׂמְחָה

Unidentified girls walk down the street during a procession on Purim in Midreshet Ben-Gurion, Israel.
Maksim Dubinsky/Shutterstock.com

Our people love to celebrate. Almost every blessing we recite (and we've got lots) praises God for something we're happy about, whether it's freedom from slavery, the food we eat, a baby's birth or a flower's scent. We bring each week to a joyous close by celebrating Shabbat; the Jewish calendar overflows with spirited holidays; and we burst with pride at our lifecycle events.

It's not surprising that we like to celebrate; most people do. But it *is* amazing that so many of our celebrations began thousands of years ago and are still going strong. Although we no longer wander the Sinai desert wearing flowing robes, we still listen to the call of the shofar on Rosh ha-Shanah, gather in a decorated booth, or *sukkah,* on Sukkot and eat matzah and bitter herbs on Passover.

Which Jewish holidays and lifecycle events do you enjoy most? Why? If you could create a new holiday, what would it be? Which Jewish historical event or value would it honor? Do you think Jewish communities around the world would still celebrate it thousands of years from now? Why or why not?

71

EXPERiENCE

LET'S CELEBRATE!

Working with a small group, share your ideas for a new Jewish holiday and brainstorm additional ideas. For each suggestion, ask yourselves why the event or value is significant and why you think Jews will continue to think so generations from now.

When your group is ready, choose one holiday from the list. Name it and write a short statement about the holiday that tells:

1. What it honors.
2. Why you think what it honors is important now and will continue to be for future generations.
3. When it is celebrated—e.g., the 12th of Elul.
4. Where it is celebrated—e.g., indoors or outdoors, at home and/or in synagogue.
5. How it is celebrated and why it includes certain rituals, special meals or foods.

Think about how to make the holiday of interest to people of all ages. Consider what might make the celebration meaningful year after year, generation after generation.

When the groups have finished their statements, have each present its holiday. Invite students to ask questions and discuss why they would or would not add the holiday to the Jewish calendar. You may even want to hold celebrations for some of the holidays!

In a modern world where many people think that new is better, why do we Jews continue to honor our ancient celebrations and rites? Perhaps it is because they are fun and inspiring and because each generation enriches the traditions with its own innovations.

Our Celebrations Are Fun

Fun is built into the core of Jewish life. It's fun to light H̲anukkah candles, play dreidel and eat latkes. It's fun to parade in Purim costumes, eat hamantaschen and drown out Haman's name with noisemakers called *ra'ashanim* (Hebrew) or *graggers* (Yiddish). And it's fun to celebrate becoming a bar or bat mitzvah—despite all the work and preparation.

Our tradition teaches that it is a mitzvah to fully enjoy each celebration or *simhah*. So we always include good food, spirited songs and guests. Chocolate coins, cheese blintzes and apples with honey are holiday symbols *and* yummy treats. Spirited singing adds delight, and the mitzvah of hospitality, or *hakhnasat orhim*, makes any *simhah* more festive with its inclusion of family and friends.

Think about a time you were a guest at a holiday or lifecycle celebration. What did your hosts do to help you feel welcome? How did their hospitality make you feel? How did you show your appreciation?

ACTIVITY

A Season and Time for Everything

Of course, not all Jewish observances are joyous. Some are times of solemn reflection and mourning. As the Bible teaches:

There is a season for everything, a time for every purpose under heaven…a time for crying and a time for laughing; a time for weeping and a time for dancing. (Ecclesiastes 3:1, 4)

What is the value of gathering as a *kehillah kedoshah* on joyous holidays *and* on holidays that commemorate tragic communal events, such as the Holocaust?

_____

_____

_____

Why do you think our tradition instructs us to also gather as a *kehillah kedoshah* when an *individual* celebrates a joyous lifecycle event or suffers a great loss like a death in the family?

_____

_____

_____

_____

EXPERiENCE

YOU'RE WELCOME

Jewish tradition teaches that extending *hakhnasat or<u>h</u>im* not only to family and friends, but also to newcomers, strangers and the poor, is at the heart of a sacred Jewish community. As the Talmud teaches, the lack of hospitality can destroy a community's good reputation: "*K'far Bish* [meaning "an evil village"] was called so because they never extended hospitality to strangers" (*Gittin* 57a).

Working in a small group, discuss the following questions:

1. Why might the people of *K'far Bish* have been reluctant to welcome strangers?

2. Why might hospitality be especially important to strangers on holidays? If you had lived in *K'far Bish*, what might you have said or done to persuade the community to be more hospitable? How might you have helped them understand that it could be fun?

3. How can your class increase the hospitality factor for new students at your school?

4. When you are ready, share your ideas with your classmates and together create a three-point action plan for increasing the hospitality factor at your school, with at least one action being focused on the celebration of Shabbat or a Jewish holiday.

Jewish tradition also teaches us to spread our good cheer by being generous and caring. That is why we contribute *tzedakah* before lighting Shabbat candles and work on mitzvah projects as part of our bar and bat mitzvah celebrations. As we see in the Scroll of Esther, weaving joy with generosity is an ancient Jewish tradition.

> The month [of Adar] was turned from a time of grief and mourning to one of gladness and joy. [Mordecai instructed] the Jews to celebrate days of feasting and fun and to send presents to friends and gifts to the poor. (Esther 9:22)

Our Celebrations Are Inspiring

IDF soldiers lights Hanukkah candles near Kibbutz Erez. ChameleonsEye/Shutterstock.com

Jewish holidays and lifecycle events inspire our people to live as a *kehillah kedoshah*. Although each celebration lasts for a limited time, the values celebrations teach are given to us for eternity. Sprinkled throughout the year, our celebrations continually inspire us to become the people we dream of being.

Shavuot and Simhat Torah (the celebrations of the giving of the Torah and the completion of its annual reading) inspire us to behave in caring, godly ways. Hanukkah and Purim remind us to live proudly as Jews, and Passover urges us to fight oppression and defend those who cannot protect themselves. Rosh ha-Shanah and Yom Kippur give us the courage to look honestly at our actions as individuals and as a community. They focus us on the choices we make and how we can improve.

And so it goes with all our holidays. Sukkot and Tu B'Shevat (the New Year of the Trees) inspire us to live in harmony with nature. Yom ha-Atzma'ut inspires our love of Israel, and Yom ha-Shoah inspires respect for the memory of the millions of Jews who were slaughtered in the Holocaust, urging us to take action so that no such tragedy happens again to *any* people.

ACTIVITY

Making Sacred Meaning

Maimonides taught, "...people who lock the doors to their courtyard and eat and drink with their families without giving anything to the poor...their meal is not the 'joy of the mitzvah' [to celebrate], but the joy of their stomachs.... This type of rejoicing is a disgrace" (*Mishneh Torah* 6:18).

Explain Maimonides's teaching in your own words.

_____

_____

_____

_____

Do you agree or disagree with Maimonides? Why or why not?

_____

_____

_____

_____

_____

75

EXPERiENCE

ROSH HODESH: AN INVITATION TO LEAVE YOUR COMFORT ZONE

Rosh Hodesh (the beginning of a new month) inspires us to move beyond our comfort zone. It asks us to renew ourselves like the moon, to enlarge our hearts and minds and to connect to our souls. It is the time to commit to developing new skills and making positive changes in our lives.

Check the Jewish (lunar) calendar to find out when the next Rosh Hodesh is. (If it's less than a week away, you may want to find the date of the following one.) Make a plan for learning a new skill or making some other positive change in your life—pitching in more at home, working on your study habits or increasing your exercise.

On Rosh Hodesh your class can conduct a celebration at which all the students demonstrate their new skills or talk about the positive changes they have made. If you like, you can work with a partner or small group to develop the skill or to make the life change. You can strengthen your sacred community by working collaboratively with your classmates, sharing your growth and being supportive of others.

Hallel, which is made up of Psalms 113–118, is recited on Rosh Hodesh. You may want to recite the opening Psalm (see below) and the *Sheheheyanu* at your celebration.

> *Halleluyah!* Offer praise, you who serve The Eternal, praise God's name. The Eternal's name will be blessed from now and for eternity (Psalm 113:1–2).

Because Rosh Hodesh celebrates the new moon's arrival, it is traditional to serve round foods, such as lentil soup, bagels and other round breads, a cheese wheel, hard-boiled eggs, nuts and fruits. You may want to include some of these at your celebration. If you do, check the dietary rules of your school and the allergies of your classmates.

Our Celebrations Are Enriched by Our Innovations

Innovation helps keep Judaism relevant to our lives. A modern Passover ritual is to place a Miriam's Cup of spring water alongside Elijah's Cup of wine to help us honor the women who have sustained our people in challenging times.

The Talmud teaches that "Moses received the Torah at Sinai and handed it down to Joshua; Joshua to the Elders; the Elders to the Prophets; and the Prophets handed it down to the Members of the Great Assembly" *(Pirkei Avot 1:1)*. In this way our tradition has been passed on from one generation to the next.

Now your generation has received the Torah and, like our ancestors, you are asked to study it, wrestle with it, enrich your life with it and contribute to our understanding of its wisdom. You are also invited to create new ways to observe the *mitzvot*. This blending of tradition with innovation is a sacred part of our heritage, passed on to us by the Rabbis along with the Torah. It helps us honor Judaism's core beliefs while creating new sources of fun, meaning and inspiration.

Just as the Rabbis created the *haggadah t*o help our people celebrate Passover, you and your generation can contribute sparks of innovation to Jewish life. For example, you might write a poem or blessing to read at your *seder*, add a fifth question to the traditional four or add an olive to the *seder* plate to symbolize Judaism's pursuit of peace, or an artichoke to symbolize interfaith families.

ACTIVITY

Sacred Community in Action: The Synagogue

Judaism teaches us how to enjoy life while making sure that others aren't left out in the cold. Sometimes this means generously inviting others to our celebrations. Other times it means providing those in need with food, shelter or clothes, comforting the lonely or visiting the sick, *bikkur ḥolim*. Yet other times it means opening our hearts and minds to all who wish to study, pray or pursue peace and justice with us.

Describe a fun or inspiring memory you have of your synagogue. Why do you value it?

_____

_____

_____

If you and your friends ran your synagogue, what would you keep as it is, and what would you change? Be prepared to discuss your reasons.

_____

_____

_____

Speaking of food, here's a story about a heavenly Shabbat meal.

One Shabbat Rabbi Joshua ben Hananiah hosted his friend, the Roman Emperor Hadrian, for dinner. It was quite an event, for it included *hallah*, vegetable soup, sweet-and-sour fish, roasted meat with potatoes, pickled salads and carob cake. After devouring generous servings of everything the emperor thanked Rabbi Joshua profusely and went home.

Back in his palace Hadrian could not forget Rabbi Joshua's heavenly meal. So he sent for the recipes, which he promptly forwarded to the court chef. But no matter how his chef prepared the meal, it always fell short of the emperor's pleasure. Frustrated, Hadrian demanded that Rabbi Joshua explain what was missing from the recipes.

"Shabbat spice," the rabbi said without hesitation.

"Tell me where I can buy some, for I must have it," responded the emperor.

"I'm afraid you cannot buy Shabbat spice, for it is free, a gift to all who honor the sacred Seventh Day," responded Rabbi Joshua. "It is Shabbat itself that flavors food with the taste of heaven." (Based on *Shabbat* 119a)

What do you think Shabbat spice is? Have you ever experienced it? If you have, describe the experience. If you haven't, what do you think it would be like, and what might help you experience it?

EXPERiENCE

ADDING HEAT TO SHABBAT SPICE

Birthdays are special. But how might you feel on your birthday if nothing special was done—no "Happy Birthday" sung, no cake, cards or gifts, no special meal or hug?

Just as birthday rituals bring out the joy and flavor of our special day, so the rituals we observe on the seventh day—our weekly birthday celebration of the world—bring out the taste of Shabbat, its special spice.

Before creating an innovation that can intensify your experience of Shabbat spice, check off the traditional ways you like to or want to celebrate the day.

- ☐ Contribute *tzedakah* before Shabbat
- ☐ Sing *Shalom Aleichem*
- ☐ Light Shabbat candles
- ☐ Recite *Kiddush* over wine and the *Motzi* over _hallah_
- ☐ Eat Shabbat meals with your family
- ☐ Host guests
- ☐ Attend Shabbat prayer services in synagogue
- ☐ Perform the *havdalah* ceremony
- ☐ Other: _____

_____

Working in small groups, discuss the Shabbat traditions that are most meaningful and enjoyable to you and why. Then brainstorm innovations that could bring out or intensify your experience of Shabbat spice. For example, on Friday night your family might have a group hug after lighting candles, or each person might share something good that happened during the week.

The best recipe for celebrating Jewish holidays and lifecycle events is to blend the ingredients of our centuries-old traditions with your soul's creative spice. This mixture of ancient and modern rituals can strengthen your *kesher* with the community and also help leave your impact on Jewish life.

EXPERIENCE YOUR SACRED COMMUNITY IN ACTION

Choose one activity.

FAMILY SPICE

Share the list of Shabbat rituals on page 79 with your family. Ask which rituals they enjoy most and express your own thoughts. Then share the innovations your class wants to observe in the coming month and ask if your family is willing to observe them as well. If they would prefer to modify the ritual or adapt it to your family's style, work together to create a compromise.

Your family may also want to develop its own innovation, which you can share with your class.

UNDER-COVER CONNECTION

We eat _hallah_ and drink wine on Shabbat and holidays such as Rosh ha-Shanah, Sukkot, Sim_h_at Torah and Shavuot. To help connect to your _kehillah kedoshah_ at those times, you and your classmates can make _hallah_ covers using the same material. You can personalize it by decorating the cover to your taste, or the class can choose words and symbols that will appear on everyone's cover.

A good size for the cover would be 15" x 20". You can paint or appliqué decorations, including Hebrew or English words. The sides can be hemmed or folded over using stitching tape.

WELCOME TO AM YISRAEL

Write a prayer for a newborn that could be read at a _brit milah_ or baby naming ceremony to express the community's hopes for the child as he or she is welcomed into the _Brit_. Your words can be a source of hope for the parents and community and an inspiration for the child as he or she grows up.

Prayer

Tefillah תְּפִלָּה

Some days anything that *can* go wrong *does*. We miss a free throw and stub our toe, splatter ketchup on a favorite shirt, lose ten dollars and our lucky charm, receive an unfair grade and get a bright red zit on the tip of our nose.

We may want to scream *"Stop!"* But we don't, and it doesn't.

Worse yet, we replay the events of the day in an endless loop in our head. Over and over we experience the disappointment and frustration, and it hurts…a lot. So how can we defuse those terrible, horrible, no good, very bad days?

Some people reach out to friends, take a walk or go for a run. Others, like Alexander of our long-ago bedtime book, favor a move to Australia. What works for you?

Wake Up and Track the Good Stuff

Like Alexander's mom, our Rabbis knew that "Some days are like that. Even in Australia." That is why prayer, or *tefillah,* reminds us that life is good, even if it's imperfect.

Without such reminders we might walk around half asleep, keeping track of what we *did not* get but not noticing all we *did* receive. Reciting blessings, or *brakhot,* and other prayers can be a good waker-upper.

ACTIVITY

Sometimes You May Need to Kvetch

Even if we know that life is good, sometimes we may need to kvetch. Sometimes we need prayers to express our disappointment and doubt, our rage and impatience, our pain and dashed hopes. At such times, spontaneously praying—silently or aloud—can calm our hearts and renew our souls.

How can we find relief in expressing the hurt we feel through prayer without saying mean-spirited things about others? Why is this important?

_____

_____

_____

_____

EXPERiENCE

AN OVERFLOWING GLASS

The author of *Alexander and the Terrible, Horrible, No Good, Very Bad Day,* Judith Viorst, often writes about life's ups and downs. Viorst is Jewish, and like our more traditional Rabbis, she reminds us that although life is imperfect, we are blessed. She believes that "Life is not about seeing the glass half empty or half full. The point is that you have a glass." In other words, like Rabbi Meir, Viorst urges us to appreciate the good we have.

Working independently or with a small group, brainstorm a list of one hundred blessings in your life, everything and everyone you are grateful for. Think about all the details that go into your happiness—each of your healthy organs and limbs; your friends, family, teachers and pets; your growing list of skills and talents; and your favorite foods, books, games and sports.

Write each item on a separate small piece of paper. Roll it up like a scroll and place it in a glass that you keep in your bedroom.

When you have a rough day or are feeling blah, you can read some of the scrolls to help you regain good feeling, then turn their words into a series of blessings. For example, you might recite the traditional Hebrew opening *(Barukh Attah Adonai, Eloheinu, Melekh ha-Olam)* and then, in English, express gratitude for what you noted on the scrolls.

You and your classmates can decorate your glasses with glass paint from a craft store. Consider including a common element—words or a design—that appears on everyone's glass to symbolize the blessing of your *kehillah kedoshah.*

Our sage Rabbi Meir suggested that we recite one hundred blessings every day, which is about one blessing every ten minutes we're awake. These blessings help track all the good in our lives—the beauty of trees, food's flavor, our friendships and our parents' love.

When we're having a rough day, blessings and other prayers can't magically erase our pain, but they can ease it with reminders of all we have to be grateful for. They can give us the calm and comfort to think more clearly and wisely about what has happened and what we need to do next.

ACTIVITY

The *Sheheheyanu*: A Blessing and a Celebration

You have already learned that we recite the *Sheheheyanu* to celebrate seeing a friend for the first time in thirty days. You may also know that we recite it on the first night of holidays such as Rosh ha-Shanah, Hanukkah and Passover, at the birth or adoption of a child and at weddings and bar and bat mitzvah celebrations.

But did you know we can recite the *Sheheheyanu* when we have a new or unusual experience we're happy about? We can recite it the first time we wear something new—jeans, a baseball cap or a suit—or celebrate a birthday, anniversary or camp reunion. Reciting the blessing can transform personal experiences into sacred moments of gratitude and joy.

Think about the past week. Was there an important moment you could have turned into a celebration by reciting the *Sheheheyanu*? Did you have a glorious first-time experience this season, like winning a club election or catching a fly ball?

In the next two weeks, consider what experience you can turn into a celebration by reciting the *Sheheheyanu*. How can reciting the blessing with your classmates strengthen your *kesher* to your sacred community and your feelings of joy and gratitude?

_____

_____

How might celebrating the joyous *Sheheheyanu* moments in your life help you handle disappointments and setbacks when they arise?

_____

_____

Share the Wealth

Prayers can remind us not only to be thankful but also to share what we have. Reciting *ha-Motzi* before a meal can be like a shofar's wake-up call to savor food *and* to feed our pet. Similarly, reciting prayers of gratitude for our health can train our mouths to smile more *and* to speak words of comfort to friends and neighbors who are sad, lonely or ill.

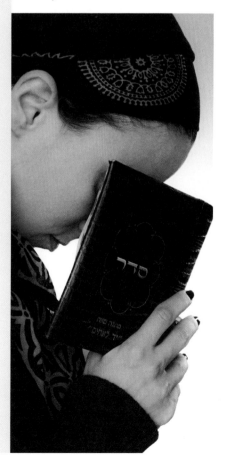

The Source of Infinite Blessing

Brakhah is the Hebrew word for "blessing." It has the same root— ב *vet,* ר *resh,* כ *khaf*—as *breikhah,* meaning "a spring." Our Rabbis teach that just as a spring constantly flows with fresh supplies of life-giving water, so God is the source of infinite blessings.

Why might this teaching encourage people to share the good fortune with which they are blessed?

_____

_____

_____

_____

_____

_____

_____

_____

_____

Prayers like the *Ashrei*, which is traditionally recited three times a day, help focus us on the care and support we receive. Psalm 145 is the heart of the prayer and includes these words:

> The Eternal supports all who stumble
> And straightens those who are bent.
> Everyone's eyes look to You with hope,
> And You provide them with food in due time.
> You open your hand
> And satisfy the needs of every living creature.

(Psalm 145:14–16)

EXPERiENCE

LET'S TALK ABOUT IT: PSALM 145:14–16

Working with a *hevruta* partner, reread the text from Psalm 145. Take turns reading it aloud. Discuss with your partner what it means to "support all who stumble" and "straighten those who are bent." Given that God is neither a person nor a force that we can see or touch, how would God do that? If the words of the psalm are true, why do some creatures suffer?

Discuss how, as a creature made in God's image (*be-tzelem Elohim*) you can perform godly acts that help make the words of *Ashrei* come true. Why might a sacred community be a powerful resource in accomplishing such tasks?

In the movie *Pay It Forward* a middle-school student seeks to make the world a better place. He responds to acts of kindness not by *paying back* the person who helped him but by *paying forward* three other people with acts of kindness. With your class, create a living *midrash* by forming a Pay It Forward action group. Invite each student to describe a blessing he or she has received from God and to pay the kindness forward to three people.

Create a Pray It Forward *brakhah* to recite on such occasions. It can express gratitude for the goodness in your life and the hope that your actions will inspire others to pay forward good deeds.

Commit to taking these actions by a specific time, perhaps within a week or two. Then reconvene your Pay It Forward action group to discuss what you did, how you felt, how people responded and why you would or wouldn't pay kindness forward again or make it into a daily habit.

We're All Included

You might think it odd or careless that even when we pray alone we say "Praised are You *our* God" and "Help *us* lie down in peace." Why don't we say *"my* God" and "Help *me*"?

In fact, it is neither odd nor careless. Rather, our prayer book, or *siddur*, reminds us that we never truly pray alone. Like the blessings that help focus us not only on our good fortune but also on the opportunities to share with others, our many prayers connect us to the larger world. They remind us that we are not alone, that we belong, that we need to reach out to receive *and* to give.

Through Me

Rabbi Harold Schulweis teaches that every time we bless God for something like making peace or feeding the hungry, we should add the words "through me." It becomes "Blessed are You....Who frees the captives through me."

What lesson does Rabbi Schulweis want to teach?

ACTIVITY

Making Sacred Meaning

The sage Hillel taught, "If I am not for myself, who is for me? And if I am only for myself, what am I?" (*Pirkei Avot* 1:14). How might his words help explain why so many of our prayers speak of "we," "us" and "our"?

_____

_____

_____

_____

Since you are included in the prayers of others, you may as well skip synagogue and play tennis. Right? *Not.*

Our prayers seek to renew and energize us both as individuals and as a *kehillah kedoshah*. They also seek to inspire us to rededicate ourselves to the ideals of the *Brit*. The more people who participate in synagogue services, the greater the odds are for our success.

Think about it. What does it feel like when the sanctuary prayer service is 20% full? What does it feel like when every seat is taken? Which of the two services is more likely to uplift and inspire you? Why?

EXPERiENCE

A CHANGE IN VOICE

To experience the difference between reciting prayers on behalf of the community and doing so just for oneself, find three blessings or other prayers in the *siddur* that refer to "us," "our" or "we." Read them as they are, then substitute the plural pronouns with "me," "mine" and "I."

Share the prayers with a partner and discuss what the benefits are of saying them each way. Tell your partner if you have a preference and why.

Say It with Meaning

Despite our best intentions, sometimes we feel distant or bored in prayer services, and our thoughts may wander. It can happen to anyone. It also can be a missed opportunity, for when sacred words are said as blah, blah, blah they lose their power to inspire.

Our prayer services are essentially conversations between the Rabbis, God and us. The Rabbis speak through the framework, or *keva*, of the *siddur*, which includes prayers like *Kaddish* and the *Amidah*. God's "voice" is heard through the Torah service and prayers built on sacred text like the *Ashrei*.

We speak through our souls.

Of course, we recite the prayers' words, but our souls personalize their meaning. That is how we simultaneously join the community in prayer *and* have our own individual experience. To help, our tradition teaches us to recite prayers mindfully, with sincerity and intention, or *kavanah*, from deep within our souls.

EXPERiENCE

PUTTING KAVANAH INTO THE KEVA

Our Rabbis taught that a prayer without *kavanah* is like a body without a soul. What do you think they meant?

You may need to try different strategies to help you engage your soul in prayer. Some people meditate before they pray, while others quiet their minds by reciting psalms. Other folks pray slowly, concentrating on each word rather than being concerned about reciting the entire prayer. Yet others find that saying the words aloud with the congregation increases their *kavanah*, even if they don't understand many of the Hebrew words. And yet other folks pray using the English translations, to make sure their understanding is complete.

To help you explore different approaches to achieving *kavanah* you are invited to recite the *Shema* in different ways.

שְׁמַע יִשְׂרָאֵל יי אֱלֹהֵינוּ יי אֶחָד.

"Listen Israel, The Eternal is our God. The Eternal alone" (Deuteronomy 6:4).

Working with your classmates, recite the prayer together in Hebrew and then in English. Discuss why you think it is considered the key statement of Jewish faith. Also discuss whether or not it feels different reciting it in Hebrew versus English and, if it does, why you think that is the case.

Now try reciting the prayer together in Hebrew but saying each word slowly, in a long single breath. Say it standing, then sitting; with your eyes open, then shut. Say it silently, then aloud. Try as many different combinations as you can think of to recite the words with deep meaning and connection to your soul. Then share your preferences with your classmates.

ACTIVITY

What's the Problem?

Rabbi Abraham Joshua Heschel taught that "The problem is not how to revitalize prayer; the problem is how to revitalize ourselves" *(Man's Quest for God)*.

Do you agree or disagree? Why?

_____

_____

_____

_____

Describe one step you can take to revitalize yourself when you pray.

_____

_____

_____

_____

_____

_____

_____

Our tradition also invites us to pray directly from our souls, without relying on the words of the *siddur*. The Hasidic stories below tell of two people who followed that path.

> A young shepherd who knew the letters of the *alef bet* but not how to read would pray by reciting the alphabet again and again with deep fervor. Occasionally he would pause to humbly say, "Dear God, I only know the letters. Please rearrange them into the correct words."

Do you think the shepherd's prayer had value? Why or why not? What lesson does his story teach?

The second story is similar but has a few different twists.

> A young shepherd came to the synagogue to pray on Yom Kippur. He was illiterate but had an extraordinary talent for whistling. Working up his courage, he whistled an exquisite song of return to God, or *teshuvah*. The other worshipers were angered and demanded that he leave or stop whistling.
>
> But the rabbi insisted that they let the shepherd be. "Until he came I could feel that our prayers were blocked from the heavenly court," said the rabbi. "Yet his whistling easily passed through, carrying our prayers straight to God."

What are the similarities between the stories? What are the differences? What do both stories teach about *kavanah?* How might the stories help you pray with *kavanah?* How might they help you become a more open-hearted and open-minded member of your *kehillah kedoshah?* Why?

EXPERiENCE

OPENING OUR HEARTS AND MINDS

Divide your class into several groups of at least three students. Each group will become a theater troupe that role-plays the second story on page 88, but with a few twists. In each troupe one student will play the shepherd, at least one will play a congregant who is annoyed by the shepherd's nontraditional form of prayer and at least one other will play a congregant who speaks up on behalf of the shepherd. Finally, the person who is the shepherd will not whistle. Instead, he or she will create another nonverbal form of prayer that expresses *kavanah*.

Before presenting the story each theater troupe can take fifteen minutes to plan its presentation and the lesson(s) it wants to teach. When you are ready, take the stage! After the troupes have made their presentations, discuss how the lessons you taught can be applied to your sacred communities—your classroom and synagogue.

ACTIVITY

Sacred Community in Action: Creating Prayer Books

Jewish tradition teaches that God wrote the Torah, but who wrote the *siddur*? The answer is lots of people, including some who haven't been born yet. The Rabbis started recording our prayers on parchment in the ninth century; we've continued editing and writing prayer books and will pass the project on to future generations. In this way the *siddur* maintains its basic structure and core set of prayers while reflecting new voices and concerns. For example, before 1948 the *siddur* had no prayer for the modern State of Israel.

Imagine that you were invited to write a new song or prayer for a *siddur*. What subject would you choose to write on? Why?

_____

_____

_____

_____

EXPERIENCE YOUR SACRED COMMUNITY IN ACTION

Choose one activity.

PARENTS CAN BE A BLESSING

It's a tradition for parents to recite a blessing over their children after lighting Shabbat candles. This week turn the tables by writing a blessing of gratitude in honor of your parent or parents. Before writing, think about the qualities and actions for which you want to express gratitude.

MEDITATION

Working as a class, create a short meditation to help you clear your mind so that before you start praying, you strengthen your *kesher* with your soul, God and the community.

The meditation can be verbal or nonverbal. It can be a melody or song, movement or breathing exercise or combination of several techniques. You may want to begin by brainstorming ideas in small groups and then convene as a class to create the meditation.

ONE GOD, MANY NAMES

Make a collage of God's many different names. For example, you might include *El*, *Elohim*, *Yaweh*, *Shaddai*, *Elyon*, *Shalom*, The Eternal, The Creator, The Place, The Rock, The Compassionate One and The Holy One. You can use either Hebrew or English names or a combination of both, and you can use Hebrew or English letters or a combination.

When you complete the collage you can show it to your class and then hang it in your room at home. It can be a reminder of the many ways in which you experience God's presence in your life and an inspiration to recite words of gratitude and to behave in godly, giving ways.

90

Peace

Shalom שָׁלוֹם

Honoring *mitzvot* such as eating matzah with bitter herbs, recycling, praying and comforting friends usually doesn't require running shoes or toned legs. However, there are two *mitzvot* that *do* require a runner's persistence and determination:

צֶדֶק צֶדֶק תִּרְדֹּף

Justice, justice pursue (Deuteronomy 16:20)

and

בַּקֵּשׁ שָׁלוֹם וְרָדְפֵהוּ

Seek peace and pursue it (Psalm 34:15).

But why isn't it enough simply to *be* just and peaceful? Why must we *pursue* justice and peace?

Let's take justice first.

Think back to Noah and Abraham. We know that Noah was a just man—both fair and trustworthy—yet he did not *pursue* justice. When things went south for the rest of humankind, Noah shrugged his shoulders and focused on himself. In contrast, Abraham not only was just, he also *pursued* justice, even when it meant standing up to God.

But what about *shalom?* What exactly is it, and why and how must we pursue it?

EXPERiENCE

WHAT DOES PEACE LOOK LIKE TO YOU?

Hand out a sheet of drawing paper to your classmates along with a variety of crayons or highlighters. You will each draw a scene that illustrates a time when you had a deep experience of peace. Perhaps it took place in your home or synagogue, at camp or on a boat. Someplace on your paper, write your definition of peace.

When everyone is ready, share your drawings and definitions. Discuss what the experience of peace is like for each of you and compare your definitions of it. Finally, discuss how you feel when peace is not present in your life.

91

The Signs of Shalom

Our Rabbis taught that *"Shalom* must be sought at all times—at home and away from home we must seek *shalom* and pursue it" *(Numbers Rabbah 19:27).* But before we can pursue *shalom* we must know what it looks like, what the signs are that it is or is not present.

Working in small groups and using the many meanings of *shalom*—peace, hello, good-bye, completeness, wholeness, health, total well-being, safety, tranquility and prosperity—brainstorm ten signs of *shalom* that can be found in a home and ten in a school.

Signs may be seen in how people talk to and treat one another. For example, why might it be a sign of *shalom*/well-being when people speak respectfully to one another? Similarly, why might it be a sign of *shalom*/safety when people are kind and show trust?

When each group has completed its list, share your ideas and discuss how the signs you noted are present or absent in your school and what you can do to strengthen the presence of *shalom*.

Pursuing Shalom Is about More than Finding Peace

Peace is the absence of war and hostility. *Shalom*—the word the Bible uses—is more complex. Of course, it is Hebrew for "peace," "hello" and "goodbye." But it also means "completeness," "wholeness," "health," "total well-being," "safety," "fulfillment," "tranquility," "prosperity" and "harmony." In short, *shalom* is the Jewish idea of perfection, the ideal state of affairs.

How's Your Shalom?

In modern Hebrew, when we greet someone we ask מַה שְׁלוֹמְךָ *Mah shlomkha?* (masculine) or מַה שְׁלוֹמֵךְ *Mah shlomeikh?* (feminine). The expression literally means, "What is your *shalom?*" In other words, we're asking, "What's going on? Are you feeling healthy, tranquil, prosperous and whole? Are you at peace?"

How do the many meanings of *shalom* compare with your definition of peace? Do health and prosperity fit in? Why or why not? Why do you think completeness and wholeness are part of *shalom?* If you were to draw a picture of it, what would *shalom* look like? How might it look different from plain peace?

Our Rabbis taught, "The whole Torah exists for the purpose of promoting *shalom*" *(Midrash Tanhuma, Shoftim 18).* Looking at the word's many meanings, how does the Torah's teaching to feed and shelter those in need and to protest bullying promote *shalom?* How can visiting those who are ill, or *bikkur holim,* and welcoming guests, or *hakhnasat orhim,* also promote our ideal?

Peace or Consequences

Families and communities are made up of individuals with unique combinations of talents, temperaments and points of view. It's what makes each of us interesting and gives us personality. But our diversity can also lead to conflict. In fact, it's impossible to completely avoid conflict with others. Our Bible heroes sure couldn't.

In their youth Jacob and Esau were often at each other's throats; Joseph's jealous brothers sold him into slavery; and Moses' unruly flock challenged him at every turn. Even so, their stories are sacred, for through them we learn to pursue peace. Jacob wrestled with his conscience; Joseph forgave his brothers; and Moses was a compassionate leader who sought harmony among *Am Yisrael*.

Shalom Is in Our Prayers

Shalom is at the core of all that is good in life and the foundation of every *kehillah kedoshah,* and so it is in our prayers throughout the week. Every time we recite the *Amidah* we pray that God will "Grant *shalom* universally, with goodness and blessing, grace and love and mercy…" And on nights when we recite the *Hashkiveinu* we ask God to "spread over us the shelter of Your *shalom.*"

Our yearning for *shalom* is also found in many others prayers, including *Birkat ha-Mazon, Kaddish* and the Priestly Blessing, which parents recite over their children on Friday nights. Perhaps the shortest (unofficial) prayer is the one we recite each time we say "Shabbat *Shalom.*" This greeting is like a shorthand blessing we offer to others.

Write a prayer that expresses your *kehillah kedoshah*'s desire for and willingness to pursue *shalom*. Be prepared to share it with the class.

_____

_____

_____

_____

ACTIVITY

Making Sacred Meaning

Rabbi Shimon ben Gamliel taught, "A person who makes peace at home is like someone who makes *shalom* in all Israel" *(Avot de Rabbi Natan 28:3).*

Why do you think our tradition teaches that making peace at home, *sh'lom bayit,* is of such great importance?

_____

_____

_____

_____

Describe two things you can do or stop doing, or words you can say or stop saying, to make your home more peaceful. Also describe why you think it would have a positive impact.

_____

_____

_____

_____

_____

_____

Yet it was Moses' brother, Aaron, whom Hillel named as the role model for pursuing peace. "Learn from Aaron, love peace and pursue it; love people and bring them close to the Torah," our sage urged *(Pirkei Avot 1:12).* Ironically, Aaron won this praise because he committed idolatry; he built the golden calf.

Here's what the Torah tells us. After the Israelites received the Ten Commandments, Moses left to receive the rest of the Torah from God. Weeks passed, but he did not return. (This meant that the newly freed slaves were now the nation with the invisible God *and* a leader they could not see. Scary!) Losing faith, the people demanded that Aaron make them a god they *could* see (like the sort they knew in Egypt).

Aaron said to them, "Remove the gold rings that are on the ears of your wives, sons and daughters and bring them to me." All the people removed the gold rings that were in their ears and brought them to Aaron. He took [the rings] from them, tied them all in a cloth and made it into a calf.

And [the people] exclaimed, "This is your god, O Israel, who brought you up out of the land of Egypt!"

When Aaron saw [this] he built an altar before it; and Aaron announced, "Tomorrow will be a festival for The Eternal." [The people] arose early the next day and offered up burnt offerings and sacrifices of *shalom*…." (Exodus 32:2–6)

EXPERiENCE

LET'S TALK ABOUT IT: EXODUS 32:2–6

Working with a _hevruta_ partner, reread the text from Exodus. Take turns reading aloud. Discuss why you think that Aaron, a loyal man of God, was willing to meet the people's demand. Why didn't he refuse or at least try to change their minds? What sentence in the text suggests that Aaron did not want to abandon God?

Our Rabbis created a _midrash_ to explain why Aaron built the golden calf. According to it, Moses had promised to return in forty days. On day forty at noon Satan made a vision of Moses appear before the Israelites. It showed their leader stretched out dead. Frightened, the people sought comfort in a false god and threatened to kill Aaron, their priest, unless he made one for them.

The Rabbis say that Aaron swiftly responded the way he did because he was worried that God would not forgive _Am Yisrael_ if they were to slay their priest. So in the hope of restoring peace, Aaron took on himself the sin of creating an idol and building an altar.

Working with your _hevruta_ partner, create a _midrash_ based on the conversation Aaron might have had with his wife Elisheva after creating the idol and altar and waiting to see what would happen at the "festival of The Eternal." With what fears and guilt might Aaron have wrestled? How might his wife have responded?

You may read your _midrash_ to the class or perform it. After all the partners have presented, discuss why you think our tradition teaches that it may be honorable to disrespect God by making an idol if you do so to pursue peace by preventing violence and the loss of human life. Discuss why our Rabbis teach "...God's name may be blotted out in water for the sake of _shalom_"

(Leviticus Rabbah 9:9).

ACTIVITY

What Destroyed the Temple?

The Talmud teaches that long after Aaron made the golden calf and the Israelites arrived in *Eretz Yisrael*, the Holy Temple was destroyed because of our ancestors' groundless hatred, or *sinat ḥinam*. Unwilling to peacefully settle their differences, they ridiculed and fought each other. Our Rabbis say that it was the lack of *shalom* among the Israelites, *not* the Romans, that destroyed our Temple and Jerusalem.

How does the Talmud's teaching help you understand why Hillel praised Aaron?

_____

_____

_____

_____

Describe two reasons why people might be unwilling to pursue *shalom*. What might you say to change their minds?

_____

_____

_____

_____

Peacefully Resolving Conflicts

Today, as in biblical times, there are no perfect individuals, families or communities, and we all experience conflict. Fortunately, perfection isn't the standard we must meet. Each of us need only do his or her best to become a peacemaker, or *rodef shalom*.

Here are a few tips to help you peacefully resolve conflicts that arise in your life.

1. **Don't hold grudges!** The Torah instructs us, "Do not hate your brother [or sister] in your heart" (Leviticus 19:17). In other words, don't let hurt or anger fester. Speak up before your concerns turn into conflicts.

2. **Speak with respect and be a good listener.** Speak in a calm and respectful tone rather than an angry or loud voice. Give others your undivided attention when they speak, permitting them to express their feelings and points of view without interruption.

3. **Don't turn the conversation into a good guy/bad guy argument.** Make solving the problem your goal, not proving who is to blame.

4. **Become partners in solving the problem.** Work together to figure out what went wrong, why it happened, how to correct the problem and how to avoid such conflicts in the future.

5. **Be open to compromise.** Winning is not about getting your own way; it is about improving your relationship. If you are flexible, your relationship may grow in trust, loyalty and respect.

6. **Agree to disagree.** Sometimes you may need to accept that although you are not adversaries, you *do* have differences of opinion. Learning to tolerate those differences may not feel comfortable at first, but it may be the best solution.

After a conflict it can be challenging to let go of resentment, anger and hurt. Yet sometimes by pursuing peace, even enemies can become friends.

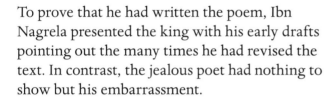

Samuel Ibn Nagrela was a Talmudic and literary scholar, a poet, a warrior and a statesman who lived in Iberia a thousand years ago when it was under Muslim rule. The story is told of a Muslim poet who, jealous of Ibn Nagrela's friendship with the Muslim king, claimed credit for writing one of Ibn Nagrela's poems.

To prove that he had written the poem, Ibn Nagrela presented the king with his early drafts pointing out the many times he had revised the text. In contrast, the jealous poet had nothing to show but his embarrassment.

Enraged, the king ordered Ibn Nagrela to punish his accuser by cutting out his tongue. But several hours later the king came upon the two poets engaged in friendly conversation. "What are you doing, Ibn Nagrela?" asked the king. "Why have you disobeyed me and now chatter with your enemy?"

"I did obey Your Majesty," responded Ibn Nagrela. "I took out my enemy's evil tongue, replaced it with one that speaks of peace and now I have a dear friend."

How might the story of Ibn Nagrela relate to your life? Have you ever peacefully settled a conflict with someone you thought of as an enemy or adversary? If you did, what helped you succeed? If you haven't had that experience, what skills do you think a *rodef shalom* would need to peacefully resolve such conflict? Why?

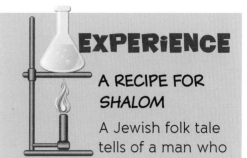

EXPERIENCE

A RECIPE FOR SHALOM

A Jewish folk tale tells of a man who went to his rabbi, saying, "I need help, for I have no *shalom*. I often respond to others with anger, arrogance and greed."

The rabbi replied, "Make this sacred recipe. Take a root of patience, a leaf of humility and a stem of generosity and mix them with branches of Torah and spring waters of justice. Cook it all in a pot of compassion, then pour it into a pitcher of understanding and drink it from a goblet of goodwill."

Divide your class into three groups. Have one group develop a recipe for becoming a *rodef shalom* at school, the second for increasing *sh'lom bayit* and the third for resolving conflicts in a synagogue community.

When the groups have completed their recipes they can share them with the class and compare their ingredients. Are any of the ingredients the same? Why do you think so? What are the differences?

ACTIVITY

Community Hero:
Yitzhak Rabin (1922–1995)

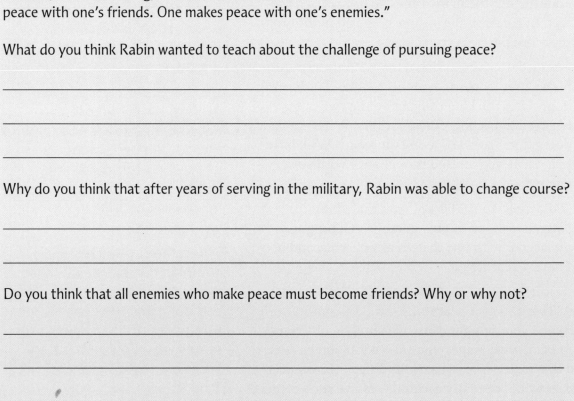

Yitzhak Rabin was a devoted member of the Israeli military for twenty-seven years. As a soldier in the Palma<u>h</u> he fought to establish the modern State of Israel, and after 1948 he became one of the country's great military leaders. Yet one day he would be honored for his commitment to pursuing peace with the very people he had once pursued in war.

In 1994, when he was Prime Minister of Israel, Rabin received the Nobel Peace Prize along with his Foreign Minister, Shimon Peres, and the President of the Palestinian National Authority, Yasser Arafat. They were honored for their work on the 1993 Israeli–Palestinian Peace Accords.

Writing about the Accords, Rabin said, "I would have liked to sign a peace agreement with Holland, or Luxembourg, or New Zealand. But there was no need to…. One does not make peace with one's friends. One makes peace with one's enemies."

What do you think Rabin wanted to teach about the challenge of pursuing peace?

_____

_____

_____

Why do you think that after years of serving in the military, Rabin was able to change course?

_____

_____

Do you think that all enemies who make peace must become friends? Why or why not?

_____

_____

_____

EXPERIENCE YOUR SACRED COMMUNITY IN ACTION

Choose one activity.

SH'LOM BAYIT

Introduce the concept of *sh'lom bayit* to your family, explaining the many meanings of *shalom*. Then share the list of tips for peacefully resolving conflicts and ask which ones your family thinks would be most helpful in your home.

Give everyone an opportunity to add his or her ideas about how to peacefully resolve conflicts. Consider posting a list in the kitchen or other family room of the ideas everyone agrees on so that you can refer to it the next time a conflict arises.

IT'S A DILEMMA

Here's a dilemma. A student in another class is bullying a classmate of yours who is afraid to speak up because the bully has threatened to become violent. How can you be an effective *rodef shalom?*

Divide the class into two or three teams to come up with peaceful solutions to the dilemma. When the groups are ready, convene as a *kehillah kedoshah* to present the solutions and discuss whether they would be practical and effective and why.

A VISION OF SHALOM

The prophet Isaiah described his vision of a world filled with *shalom*: "Nation will not raise sword against nation; never again will they know war.... The wolf will live with the lamb, and the leopard will lie down with the kid..." (Isaiah 2:4, 11:6).

As a class, discuss Isaiah's vision, including the symbolism of the animals. Then plan and create a mural to illustrate his vision and enrich it with your own ideas. When the mural is completed you may want to seek permission to exhibit it in a public area of your school.

Sacred Study

Talmud Torah תַּלְמוּד תּוֹרָה

EXPERiENCE

NO DANGER:
CONSTRUCTION GOING ON

Judaism teaches that a good argument builds trust and brings people together, helps us learn and draws us closer to truth; a bad one distances people, misleads and is hurtful. The first type of argument is considered constructive, educational and sacred; the second is considered destructive and unholy.

Working in small groups, develop five tips for conducting a good argument. Then present the list to the class, explaining why each tip can help make arguments tools for learning and for strengthening trust and friendship.

After everyone has presented, note if certain tips appear in all the groups. Then work as a class to create a list of the Top Ten Tips for Having a Good Argument and discuss how each can strengthen your *kehillah kedoshah*.

Our people are always looking for a good argument, even when we're pursuing peace. Determined to fulfill the *Brit,* we study Torah, questioning and debating its teachings, turning every word upside down and inside out until we make meaning and find truth.

Some of our greatest arguments have been recorded as sacred text in the Bible and Talmud. You have read about a few—Abraham's back-and-forth with God regarding the fate of Sodom, the daughters of Zelophehad's dispute over God's laws of inheritance and Rabbi Yohanan's arguments with his beloved *hevruta* partner, Reish Lakish.

What is the value of a *good* argument? How can it strengthen our minds, hearts and friendships? What distinguishes a good argument from a bad one?

For Heaven's Sake!

Our tradition teaches that a good argument can be a great teacher, for it can deepen our understanding of Torah and honor God. Therefore, we say such arguments are "for Heaven's sake," or *le-sheim Shamayim*.

Not only did our Rabbis argue mightily with one another *le-sheim Shamayim*, but like Abraham, they argued with God, and sometimes they won!

A famous legend teaches that Rabbi Eliezer disputed a point of Jewish law, or *halakhah*, with his colleagues. After several unsuccessful attempts to persuade them that he was right, even calling forth miraculous signs in support of his argument, Rabbi Eliezer said:

> "If *halakhah* agrees with me, let Heaven prove it."

> In response a heavenly voice called out, "Jewish law agrees with Rabbi Eliezer."

> On hearing God's declaration, Rabbi Joshua arose and said *Lo va-shamayim hi!* "The Torah is not in heaven!" (Deuteronomy 30:12). For the Torah was given to the Jewish people at Mount Sinai.

> Some time later Rabbi Natan met the prophet Elijah and asked about God's reaction to Rabbi Joshua's statement. Elijah said, "God smiled, saying, *Nitzhuni banai. Nitzhuni banai.* 'My children have defeated me. My children have defeated me.'" *(Baba Metzia 59 a–b)*

What did Rabbi Joshua mean when he said "The Torah is not in heaven"? Do you think Rabbi Joshua's argument was "for Heaven's sake"? Why or why not? Based on the legend, what do you think was our Rabbis' view of Torah study? Why?

The Root of the Meaning

Why did God repeat the closing response? Some commentators suggest that the second time it should be translated as "My children have made me eternal," because the Hebrew word for eternal, נֵצַח *netzah,* is based on the same root letters—נ *nun*, צ *tzadi* and ח *het*—as נִצְחוּנִי *nitzhuni*, meaning "[they] have defeated me."

How might good arguments about the Torah help make God and God's teachings eternal?

_____

_____

_____

Do you think that when our patriarch Abraham negotiated with God for the sake of the innocent of Sodom he was a source of divine joy like Rabbi Joshua? Why or why not?

_____

_____

_____

EXPERiENCE

IT'S DEBATABLE

According to an ancient *midrash*, before humans were created, God's angels held a debate (Genesis Rabbah 8:5). One group of angels argued that God should create humans because we would perform acts of love. The other group argued that God should not because we would be troublesome.

In the legend about Rabbi Eliezer, Rabbi Joshua insists that God has no say in the Rabbis' argument because the Torah was given to our people and is ours to study and interpret. Your class will create a *midrash* set in the hours before God gave us the Torah at Sinai. You will form two teams of angels who will debate: Should humans be given the Torah and the authority to study and interpret it? One team will argue in favor; the other will argue against.

The teams will be given time to prepare. To begin the debate each team will make an opening statement. Then they will offer rebuttals to each other's claims. Time the openings and rebuttals, giving each team about two or three minutes. The teams can have up to four rounds of rebuttals. Your teacher or a guest can judge who won.

Enjoy yourselves and have a good argument for Heaven's sake! When you are done discuss which of the Top Ten Tips for Having a Good Argument were used.

A Community Affair and a Personal Responsibility

Tradition teaches that the Torah was revealed to our people as a community at Mount Sinai. In that same spirit and tradition we are asked to study Torah as a *kehillah kedoshah* with our families, friends, teachers, classmates and rabbis.

Our Rabbis tell us that every Jewish soul that ever was or will be received the Torah at Sinai, and we each received God's instructions to:

> Take to heart these words that I command you today. Teach them to your children. Speak of them when you are at home and when you are away, when you lie down and when you rise. (Deuteronomy 6:6–7)

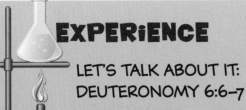

EXPERiENCE

LET'S TALK ABOUT IT: DEUTERONOMY 6:6–7

Working with a _hevruta_ partner, reread the text from Deuteronomy. Take turns reading aloud. Discuss what the implications are of the instruction to speak about the Torah everywhere and throughout the day and to teach it to the next generation. How do the instructions make it clear that _talmud Torah_ is every Jew's responsibility? How do they make it clear that _talmud Torah_ is meant to be done in community with others?

Working with your _hevrutah_ partner, create a _midrash_ about running into someone whose soul you stood next to when the Torah was given at Sinai. Your _midrash_ can describe how your souls felt when they first received the Torah, then thousands of years later what it feels like to study, interpret and live its lessons as flesh-and-blood people in twenty-first–century North American communities.

When everyone is ready you may read or perform your _midrash_ for the class. Discuss why the souls' thoughts, experiences and feelings might have changed over the centuries and what might have stayed the same and why.

Talmud Torah Is Not a One-Shot Affair

Receiving the Torah at Sinai was just the first of many sacred lessons we receive. A Talmudic _midrash (Niddah_ 30b) says that an angel teaches us the entire Torah as we develop in the womb. Then, at the very moment we are to be born, that same angel touches us right above the upper lip, pushing us into life and causing us to forget all we learned.

The Rabbis tell us that we are taught Torah in this way to make it part of our hearts and minds, and we are caused to forget what we learned so that we can fully experience the reward of studying Torah throughout our lives.

> As the sage Ben Bag-Bag said, "Turn [the Torah] over and over, for everything is in it. Think deeply about it, grow gray and old with it and do not turn away from it, for there is no greater good" (_Pirkei Avot_ 5:22).

How might studying Torah throughout your life deepen and mature your understanding of its lessons?

_____

_____

_____

ACTIVITY

Community Hero: Rebecca Gratz (1781–1869)

Rebecca Gratz was a visionary. At a time when there were few models for Jewish education in a free and open society, Gratz developed the concept of the Jewish Sunday school.

The Jewish schools in Eastern Europe, where many American Jews emigrated from, were led and taught by men who educated boys, held classes six days a week and conducted them primarily in Yiddish. In contrast, Gratz's school—the Hebrew Sunday School Society of Philadelphia, founded in 1818—was primarily led and taught by women who educated boys *and* girls, held classes once a week and conducted them in English.

Gratz's goal was to provide the community's children with the benefits of *talmud Torah* and to help them integrate their Jewish identities and traditions with their lives as Americans. She taught her students that they could play dreidel *and* team sports and celebrate Sukkot *and* Thanksgiving. Gratz lived and worked in Philadelphia, but her vision and leadership had a strong impact on Jewish education throughout North America.

Given that the majority of American Jews came from countries where they were forced to live separately from the rest of society, why were Gratz's vision and contributions of such importance?

_____

_____

_____

_____

_____

_____

_____

Great and Greater

Our Rabbis were practical people. The same Rabbis who encouraged us to recite one hundred blessings a day *and* to attend prayer services taught us to pray in buildings with windows. As important as frequent prayer is, the Rabbis didn't want us to lose sight of the larger world and of our responsibilities beyond the synagogue walls—feeding our families, being good citizens and helping the elderly, sick and poor. Praying is a *mitzvah*, but so is earning a living, loving your family, paying taxes and helping those in need.

That same mentality led our Rabbis to stress the practical value of *talmud Torah*. The Talmud says that Rabbi Tarfon and Rabbi Akiva were at a gathering of elders when the question arose:

> "What is greater, *talmud Torah* or action, the performing of *mitzvot*?"
>
> Tarfon responded, "Action is greater."
>
> "Study is greater," argued Akiva.
>
> In the end the assembly agreed that study is greater because it leads to action. *(Kiddushin 40b)*

ACTIVITY

Sacred Community in Action: Your Classoom *Kehillah Kedoshah*

You and your classmates have studied Torah, engaging in good arguments and wrestling with sacred questions. You have helped one another to find meaning in Jewish values and ethics and to clarify your own beliefs. Together you read *midrash* and made *midrash*, explored our ancient tradition and its ability to adapt, and you enriched it and the community with your own ideas.

Your growing wisdom and experience helped you form caring friendships and partnerships. You pursued *tzedek* and *shalom*, collaborating on projects that had an impact at home, in school and synagogue, in the larger world and on you.

You paid forward and prayed forward, and you built a *kehillah kedoshah* that is respectful, responsible and strong. All this need not come to an end with the coming of summer or the celebration of becoming a bar or bat mitzvah. Instead, may you enjoy new experiences, challenges and celebrations that bring your sacred community together again and again.

May you go from strength to strength! Amen.

EXPERIENCE YOUR SACRED COMMUNITY IN ACTION

Choose one activity.

SPEAK OF TORAH AT HOME

Take to heart the sacred instruction to speak about Torah at home. For example, you might lead your family in a discussion of a controversial subject that came up in your class. Before you start, share the Top Ten Tips for Having a Good Argument and then invite your family members to offer their points of view on the subject while making good use of the tips.

TEACH CHILDREN

Take to heart the instructions to teach Torah to the next generation. For example, independently or with a group, write and illustrate a Bible story for children, perhaps doing it in a scroll format. Then volunteer to read it to a class of younger students and to lead a discussion about the story's lesson. Encourage the students to talk about experiences they have had that are related to the lesson.

SPEAK WORDS OF TORAH WHEN YOU'RE AWAY FROM HOME

Take to heart the instructions to speak of Torah when you are away from home. At school you can tape together several pieces of butcher paper to create a large scroll. Working as a class, draw words or illustrations that describe sacred actions an individual or a sacred community can take to help fulfill the *Brit*. When you complete the scroll, discuss which actions you took this year and which ones you look forward to taking in the future and why.